CELTIC CROSS STITCH

CELTIC CROSS STITCH

Over 40 small, exciting and innovative projects

ANNE ORR & LESLEY CLARKE

NEW HOLLAND

First published in 2001 by
New Holland Publishers (UK) Ltd
London · Cape Town · Sydney · Auckland

Garfield House, 86 Edgware Road
London W2 2EA
United Kingdom

80 McKenzie Street
Cape Town 8001
South Africa

Level 1, Unit 4, 14 Aquatic Drive
Frenchs Forest, NSW 2086
Australia

218 Lake Road
Northcote, Auckland
New Zealand

1 3 5 7 9 10 8 6 4 2

ISBN 1 85974 641 1

Editor: Gillian Haslam
Design: Peter Crump
Photographer: Shona Wood
Production: Caroline Hansell

Editorial Direction: Rosemary Wilkinson

Reproduction by Modern Age Repro House Ltd.
Printed and bound in the U.S.A

Photographic credits:
Page 7: Janet and Colin Bord/Fortean Picture Library
Page 14: © The British Museum, London
Page 40: Werner Forman Archive/
© The British Museum, London
Page 56: The Board of Trinity College Dublin
Page 82: Allen Kennedy/Fortean Picture Library

ACKNOWLEDGEMENTS

We would like to thank all the staff at Textile
Heritage Collection for their patience during the
writing of this book.

Also, special thanks for stitching some of the
projects to Shirley Alexander, Alison Cran,
Joyce Halliday and Barbara Matthews.

CONTENTS

Introduction 6
Practicalities 8

WATER

FIRE

AIR

EARTH

INTRODUCTION
The Celtic Background

The familiar idea of the Celtic world is of a mysterious pagan people producing wondrous designs of knots and spirals, or of an Irish monk in a remote monastery poring over a beautiful illustrated bible. Both these images are just part of a story which covers many centuries and many countries.

The earliest recognizable Celtic culture appeared at about 500 BC in Europe. The Celts were a people on the move. At its height, the influence of Celtic tribes spread from Asia Minor to northernmost Scotland. When the Celts were conquered first by the Romans and then by the Anglo-Saxons, they retreated to the 'Celtic fringes' of the British Isles and Brittany, in France. From a heartland in Ireland, Christian missionaries set out to bring their distinctive Celtic Christianity to England and Scotland, and may even have voyaged as far as America. However, by 1000 AD Viking raids brought an end to the active period of Celtic history.

Through these centuries, Celtic art was influenced by the many peoples with whom the Celts came into contact, from the ancient Egyptians to the Vikings. Their early culture was not a written one, but was kept alive by a rich store of myths passed on to each generation by bards, and by the beautiful artefacts made by skilled craftsmen. It was a pagan culture of gods and warriors, of mysterious spirits forever changing their shapes, and of the watery underworld of their gods. It was also a harsh world of struggle against the earthly enemies of the elements and warring tribes, and the spiritual dangers of mysterious forces and gods. Later, the Celts showed their characteristic ability to absorb many of their existing pagan traditions into Christianity. A rich monastic and missionary culture flowered in the so-called Dark Ages, culminating in the beautiful illuminated Celtic gospels.

This rich Celtic tradition of images and stories has continued to provide inspiration, and we have certainly found it a fascinating source of designs for this book. We have divided this book into four sections, which take their inspiration from the four elements, which would have been central to the life of the Celts – Water, Fire, Air and Earth. We have used each of these four elements to explore in cross stitch the rich myths and images of the Celtic world. At the beginning of the book is a practical section which describes in detail the materials and techniques which are appropriate to all the sections of the book.

Each chapter features a range of practical projects. None of the projects is very large or complicated, but if you have never attempted cross stitch before, it makes sense to start with a simple project, such as a card, on a 14 count fabric. It is important, whether you are a beginner or an experienced cross stitcher, to read through the practical section before you start. Some of our methods may differ slightly from those you are familiar with, but we would recommend them to you for working the projects. For example, we love rich, dense colour and often use three strands of embroidery thread on a 14 count fabric. This creates the rich, glowing colours of a Celtic illuminated manuscript, but still gives a good balance between the thread and the background fabric.

The great pleasure of cross stitch is that one simple stitch is used to create beautiful and intricate designs. You do not require a lot of expensive equipment. To get started you just need a piece of fabric, a needle and thread. Work your way from simple projects to more complicated ones, from larger count fabric to the finer projects on linen. When you have worked a number of the projects, following the advice in the practical section closely, you will find that as well as creating some beautiful cross stitch, you will also have mastered all the necessary cross stitch skills, and we hope that you will go on with confidence to produce your own designs.

PRACTICALITIES

All the embroidery materials and equipment used in the projects that follow, plus the finishing materials and equipment, can easily be obtained from good needlework shops, craft stores or by mail order. We have listed some sources in the Suppliers' section on page 111.

The projects are all graded according to ease of stitching – ✳ indicates the easiest projects, ✳✳ medium skill, and ✳✳✳ projects for experienced stitchers.

FABRICS

We have used a variety of blockweave and evenweave fabrics as described below. Most of the colours we have used are easily obtained, but for ease of identification, the manufacturer's code for each colour is listed at the end of the book, on page 106.

Blockweave is woven and counted in blocks, and usually one stitch is worked over one block. Aida is a blockweave fabric.

Blockweave

Evenweave is woven and counted in threads, and, as the name suggests, has the same number of threads woven horizontally and vertically per inch. Usually one stitch is worked over two threads, except for very fine work, where one stitch is worked over one thread. Linen is an evenweave fabric.

Fabric count refers to the number of holes per inch of the fabric (hpi): the higher the number the smaller the stitch. However, when stitches are worked over two blocks or threads, the number of stitches per inch will be half the fabric count. For example, 28 count worked over two blocks gives 14 stitches per inch.

Aida fabric: A firm, easy to use blockweave fabric, which can be worked without a hoop. Our projects use 11, 14, 16 and 18 count Aida fabric.

Aida band: This is manufactured in strips with decorative woven edges. It has the same construction as Aida fabric, but a softer feel. It is available in various widths and colours. The overall count is 15, and each width of band has a maximum number of blocks (or stitches) that can be worked. We have used 3.5 cm (1½ inch) band with 14 blocks, 5 cm (2 inch) band with 26 blocks, and 8 cm (3 inch) band with 42 blocks.

Binca fabric: A 6 count blockweave fabric. It is ideal for children to use, or if you want to work a large-scale project quickly.

Evenweave fabric: Our projects use 27 and 28 count fabrics in linen or man-made fibres, such as 'Meran'. It is best worked with a hoop.

Waste canvas: This is used to stitch a design onto a non-embroidery fabric by providing a 'grid' to stitch through. The waste canvas is tacked onto the fabric and the cross stitching is worked through both layers. When the embroidery is finished, the threads of the

Evenweave

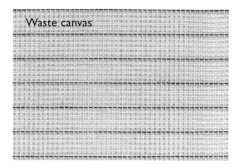

Waste canvas

canvas are dampened to loosen the glue holding them together, and they can then be gently pulled out. Waste canvas comes in various counts – here we've used 14 count.

STRANDED EMBROIDERY THREADS

We have used just two embroidery threads for the projects in this book: DMC 6-strand embroidery thread and DMC metallic thread. They both consist of six divisible strands, which are separated out into the number of strands required for the project. The individual projects also specify the number of skeins you will need of each colour, but smaller items will only use a small amount of each skein.

Anchor or Madeira threads may be substituted, using a conversion chart. If you have difficulty obtaining metallic threads, substitute a 6-strand embroidery thread in a similar colour.

NEEDLES

Tapestry needles have a rounded point, which will not damage the fabric as you work, and a large eye. The projects in this book use sizes 22, 24 and 26. The smaller the number, the larger the needle.

OTHER EQUIPMENT

Scissors: Use dressmaking or general purpose scissors for cutting pieces of fabric, and small embroidery scissors with fine points for cutting threads. Make sure your scissors are sharp.

Embroidery hoop: This is useful as it holds the weave of the fabric even and under tension, but do not stretch the fabric too tightly in the hoop. Reposition it within the hoop as you work, so that the stitching area remains centred. To avoid permanently creasing the fabric, always take the hoop off when you are not working. The two individual rings of traditional hoops can be bound with thin strips of fine fabric to improve their grip. Also available are spring hoops which are quick and easy to use.

Stitch unpicker: Ideal for correcting mistakes, but use carefully to avoid damaging the fabric.

Ruler or tape measure: The projects generally have a starting point measured in from the edges of the piece of fabric, so a ruler is indispensable.

FINISHING MATERIALS AND EQUIPMENT

Sharp needle: Use for hand sewing and for working with waste canvas.

Large-eyed needle: Use to thread ribbons, tassels etc through the embroidery fabric.

Sewing thread: Choose a colour to match the fabric project as closely as possible. For small areas of hand sewing, some projects specify using a single strand of the embroidery thread, so extra sewing thread may not be required.

Sewing machine: We have used a sewing machine to assemble cushion projects. If you do not have access to a machine, they can be hand sewn.

Sewing fabrics and trimmings: As with sewing threads, always try to source a colour that will complement your project.

Lining and backing fabrics: Use a fine, but firmly woven fabric.

Tassels and cords: If you find it difficult to purchase these, use our instructions to make your own tassels. (See the making up instructions for the Bird-headed Triskele Scissor Keep on page 79.) Cords can easily be made simply by plaiting several lengths of embroidery thread together.

Buttons, felt, ribbons, stuffing, embroidery project blanks and ready-made embroidery backgrounds are listed in the individual projects.

Craft knife and steel rule: Use these to make your own cards, tags and mounts. Make sure the knife is sharp and replace the blade when necessary.

Masking tape: Use this to attach the fabric to the back of a card or mount. Choose a width appropriate to the project. Masking tape can also be used to bind the cut edges of fabric before you start working, to prevent fraying.

Double-sided tape: Use for small projects to secure the fabric to the backing.

Stick glue: Make sure that the glue is suitable for use on fabrics and apply sparingly.

Mounting and framing materials: Requirements are listed in the individual projects. Card and mounting board are available in a wide range of colours. Ready-made cards, boxes, mounts and frames can also be bought at good stationers. Two ounce wadding is ideal for padding pictures.

WORKING TECHNIQUES

GENERAL DO'S AND DON'TS

* Keep your work clean. Always wash your hands before starting to stitch.
* Store your work rolled (not folded) in a bag.
* Always work in a good light – daylight is best. Otherwise a good lamp fitted with a daylight bulb prevents eye strain.
* Working with dark fabrics is easier if you place a light coloured cloth on your lap to show up the holes in the fabric.
* There are a variety of magnifiers suitable for working cross stitch. Test them to find one to suit your needs.

THE FABRIC

Cut the fabric with dressmaking scissors to the size of fabric specified for each project. It is then very simple to measure out the starting point. Iron the fabric before you start, if it is crumpled. The manufacturer's fold on many fabrics can be difficult to iron out, so try to cut the fabric to avoid this fold.

The fabric edges can be bound to prevent them fraying as you work. This is particularly advisable for larger projects, as the fabric will be handled a lot. Oversew the edges by hand or with a sewing machine, or bind them with masking tape.

Stitch a small knot of thread at the top edge of the fabric to mark the top of the design – if the design is symmetrical, there is never any doubt about which way you should be working.

THE CHART

Each symbol on the chart is one cross stitch on the fabric (Figs 1a and b). Each symbol represents a thread colour. If there is no symbol beside a colour name, that colour is used only for backstitch. Empty squares on the chart are background fabric. Each chart is surrounded by a numbered border counted out from, or near, the start point to aid counting. Thicker lines on the chart indicate every tenth square, and also make counting easier. Heavy black lines on the chart

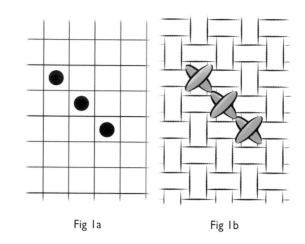

Fig 1a   Fig 1b

indicate backstitches and longstitches. Some charts also use dotted lines, to distinguish between different backstitch colours.

The starting point for stitching is indicated by an arrow, and should be used with the measurements provided in the text. Dotted lines are also used to indicate where the fabric should be cut, folded or mounted. Sometimes other general finishing details are indicated on the chart. If you wish, photocopy the chart so it can be marked without damaging the book. It can also be enlarged on a photocopier.

THE THREADS

Organise the threads before you start a project. Identify each thread with its chart symbol. Either tape a snippet of each colour beside the corresponding chart symbol on a photocopy, or buy or make a thread organiser. To make one, punch a series of holes in a long strip of stiff card. Mark the thread colour, number and symbol beside each hole, and loop through cut lengths of the corresponding thread.

Cut the threads into suitable lengths before starting to stitch. A common mistake is to assume that longer threads save time rethreading your needle. They don't, they just lead to worn thread and tangles. For 6-strand embroidery thread use 40 cm (16 inch) cut lengths. As metallic thread is brittle, use shorter lengths, not more than 35 cm (14 inches) long, and keep the eye of the needle towards the end of the thread, as it will tend to damage the thread at this point. Sometimes strands of different colours are used in the same length. These mixes are used for subtle colour effects.

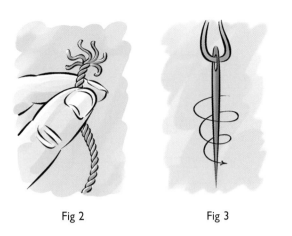

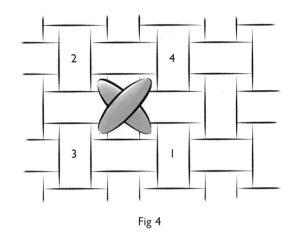

Fig 2   Fig 3

Fig 4

Separate the 6-strand threads into the number of threads required for cross stitch or backstitch in the project, by pulling them gently apart (Fig 2). If you have cut uniform thread lengths it is easy to regroup spare strands together.

The thread will twist as you are working and this can lead to tangles. Regularly let the thread and needle hang loose, so that the twist can spin out (Fig 3).

STITCHING

Try to work with an even tension. Don't pull the thread too tight, or leave it as a slight loop on the front of the work. Don't carry the thread very far across the back of the work. Work in small blocks of one colour at a time, and neatly trim away any excess thread at the back before starting another colour. It is useful to have several needles threaded ready with separate colours. Always take the needle in and out of the work in separate movements. Never try to make an in-and-out movement with your needle at the same time, as the resulting stitches will be uneven.

Never knot thread to start or finish. Begin by leaving a 3 cm (1 inch) length at the back of the fabric, and secure by working the first few stitches over it. To finish, take the thread to the back and thread it through a few nearby stitches, away from plain areas of fabric, before cutting it off. Further threads are started by weaving through the back of existing stitches.

CROSS STITCH

Use the number of strands specified in the project. Cross stitch is worked by bringing the needle up from the back of the fabric to the front at the bottom right

of a block (Fig 4). Insert the needle at the top left of the block. Bring the needle up again at the bottom left and insert at the top right to complete the cross stitch.

You may prefer to make your individual stitches in the opposite order (bottom left, top right, bottom right, top left) – either is correct. However, it is very important that whichever way you choose, you always make the top diagonals in the same direction, otherwise the work will look untidy (Fig 5).

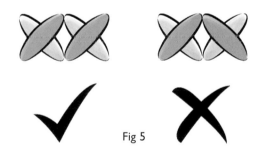

Fig 5

Horizontal rows of cross stitch are worked by stitching across a row, to make the first diagonals, and then stitching back to complete the top diagonals (Fig 6).

Fig 6

11

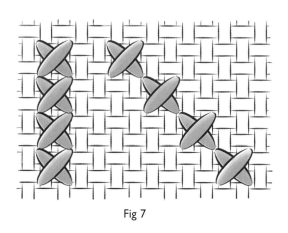

Fig 7

Working cross stitch over two threads or blocks

This technique is used for finer count fabrics. Count over two threads or blocks (rather than one) to make each stitch (Fig 7). Each complete stitch occupies nine holes in the fabric.

Part cross stitches

Partial stitches are used to create finer detail, or to round off a curved edge. They are represented on the chart by a smaller symbol in one corner of a square, or two symbols in the same chart square (Figs 8 and 9). They are worked as a three-quarter stitch, which has one complete diagonal, plus a part diagonal which is only worked into the centre of the block, rather than right across it. Alternatively, a second

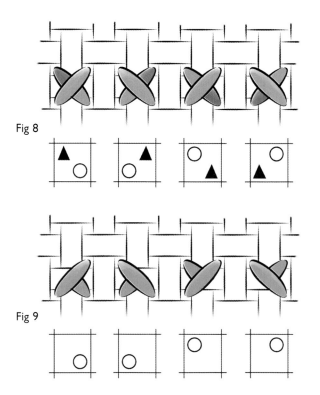

Fig 8

Fig 9

colour may be used as a quarter stitch, to complete this part diagonal.

If two colours are used in the one block, choose the more appropriate of the two colours for the three-quarter stitch. If the project is worked over two threads or blocks, the part diagonals will be worked into the centre hole of the nine that form the complete cross stitch.

Backstitch

Backstitch is used for outlining areas and for details. It is indicated by thick black, and occasionally, dotted lines on the chart. Normally it is worked after the cross stitching is complete. Use the number of strands of thread specified in the project.

Bring the needle to the front of the work one hole ahead of the starting point. Make a stitch back to this point. Bring the needle out again one hole ahead of the last completed stitch and repeat (Fig 10).

Backstitch can be worked diagonally. Single backstitches may be used as accents. A backstitch may be worked across part of a block only, for very fine detail.

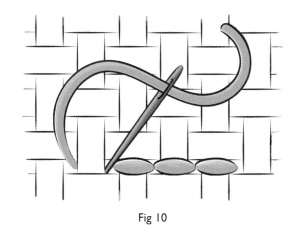

Fig 10

Longstitch

Always use the number of strands of thread specified in the project. It is a single stitch worked across more than one block. It is also indicated on the chart by a thick black line. It is sometimes used with backstitches for outlines.

CORRECTING MISTAKES

Unpick any mistakes carefully. A few stitches may be removed using the needle tip or a stitch unpicker to pull out the threads. Do not re-use unpicked thread.

If you need to remove a number of stitches, cut the top of each stitch carefully using just the tip of the embroidery scissors, and remove the threads from the back of the work. Any remaining thread fluff can be removed by patting the work gently with a piece of sticky tape.

FINISHING TECHNIQUES

Iron the finished embroidery carefully on the back on top of a thick towel with a warm iron. This prevents the stitches being crushed. Pull the design gently into shape as you iron. If necessary, the embroidery can be squared up with pins and a ruler. When making up the projects, always iron on the back of the work, or on the plain back of a project if it is made of two layers.

If the work is soiled, it may be gently hand-washed with a mild soap, patted dry in a towel and ironed completely dry on a thick towel with a cloth on top for further protection.

Carefully trim away any excess thread on the back of the work, as it may show though plain areas of fabric when the project is made up. Excess fabric should be trimmed away, but never trim very close to the stitching, as embroidery fabric frays easily, and your work could be spoiled. Leave a selvedge of 1-2 cm (½-1 inch) depending on the size of the project and how likely the fabric is to fray.

Mitring corners

Mitred corners are made by trimming slightly across the corner(s) of the finished piece diagonally. Mitre the corners if two pieces of work are being stitched together, and turned right sides out, as the corners will be flatter. But again, never mitre too close to a stitched corner, as the movement of turning the fabric to the right side will cause fraying.

Adding trimmings

When adding trimmings (tassels, ribbons, etc) to an embroidery, never cut into the body of the fabric. To thread a trimming through the work, use either a large-eyed needle or a crochet hook. Tease open a hole in the fabric as wide as possible and carefully thread the trimming through.

Making cards and tags

We have given the specific cut size of the card required in each project. Cards are then scored and folded to the finished size. You can use a different size card (either made or purchased), but do check that the size is appropriate for the embroidery.

Mounts and frames

The aperture position of the mount is indicated on the chart by a dotted line. As individual stitching tension varies, the aperture size given is for guidance only and should be checked against your own work. If you buy a bevelled mount, check the effect of the bevel on the aperture size. The overall size of the mount or frame should complement the stitched design. Acid-free mounting board will protect the embroidery.

The embroidery is secured to the back of the mount using wide masking tape. Make sure the fabric is centred and taut. Alternatively, lace the embroidery around the mount board (Fig 11). Iron it around the mount, with an optional centre piece of wadding, fold in the corners, pin the fabric in position on the sides of the mount and, using a strong thread, lace the opposite sides together

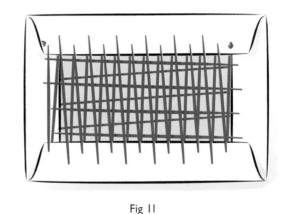

Fig 11

It is an individual choice whether or not to use glass in the frame. It protects the embroidery from dirt, but the glass does make the details of the embroidery less easy to see. Non -reflective glass will cut down on the problem of reflected light. Glass should always be mounted in the frame, so that it does not touch and crush the stitching.

Other specific finishing details are given within the individual projects.

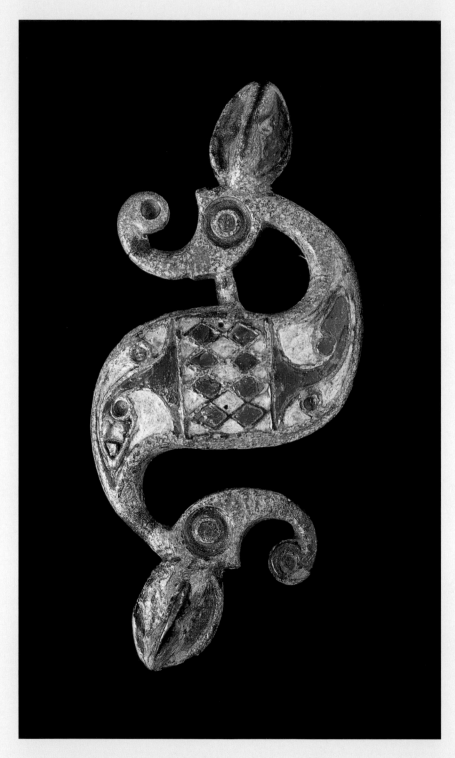

Sea serpents guarded the entry to the Celtic otherworld beneath the sea.

WATER

For the Celts, water was the most important element. As it flowed, it healed and purified. The otherworld of the spirits and the afterlife were thought to be below lakes or beneath the sea, guarded by serpents. Guardian spirits lived in wells and springs and were sacred places of pilgrimage. Fish had magical properties, later reinforced by the use of a fish as the symbol of Christ. The sea provided passage to other lands and a rich harvest of food, but it could be unpredictable and dangerous to man, and had to be placated with gifts.

THE DESIGNS

Many Celtic designs are built up from a number of elements, with a central image often surrounded by a variety of elaborate borders, creating a complex whole. The so-called 'carpet pages' of illuminated manuscripts show this process of design at its most beautiful and complex. In this chapter, we have used repeating images and borders to create different designs. For example, a simple  salmon shape, taken from a small detail in the *Book of Kells*, is used in different combinations of its own image and with added borders to create several projects. We have 'cheated' in that the corners of the borders are simple squares, which make it easy for you to extend the designs if you wish. Once you have worked these projects, it is fun to try constructing your own Celtic border patterns.

CONNLA'S WELL SCENTED PILLOW

Many salmon of knowledge lived peacefully in the secret setting of Connla's Well. When the maiden Boann trespassed on this sacred place to discover the secret of their magic powers, the salmon deserted the well and swam away to become the river Boyne.

Level ✳✳✳. The stitched design is 84 x 84 stitches, approximately 15.5 x 15.5 cm (6 x 6 inches). Each stitch in this design is worked over TWO threads.

YOU WILL NEED:

* Fabric: 27 count evenweave fabric in turquoise, 30 x 70 cm (12 x 28 inches)
* Tapestry needle: size 26 and a sharp sewing needle
* Sewing thread: in turquoise to match fabric
* Lining fabric
* Stuffing
* Pot pourri
* Threads: DMC 6-strand embroidery thread in the following colours and quantities:

Symbol	Colour	Shade	Skeins
▲	Tan	920	2
⊠	Green	907	2
⊡	Yellow	445	1

STITCHING INSTRUCTIONS

Preparation: Cut the fabric into three pieces: one piece 30 x 30 cm (12 x 12 inches) for the front, and two pieces 20 x 30 cm (8 x 12 inches) for the back. Oversew or bind the edges of the large square so it does not fray while being embroidered.

Cross stitch: Use two strands of the embroidery thread and work each stitch over TWO threads.

Backstitch: Use one strand of tan for the salmon details, except for the tail tips which are worked with two strands of tan thread at the same time as the cross stitch.

Starting point: This is indicated on the chart overleaf by an arrow. The first stitch is made at a point 7 cm (3 inches) from the right-hand side and 7 cm (3 inches) from the bottom of the front square of fabric.

MAKING UP

Make up this cushion in the same way as the Swimming Salmon cushion on page 19, except that the central square is 3 cm (1¼ inches) from the embroidered border. Make an inner cushion with the lining fabric. This prevents the pot pourri oils damaging your fabric. Stuff the inner cushion pad with a mixture of stuffing and pot pourri.

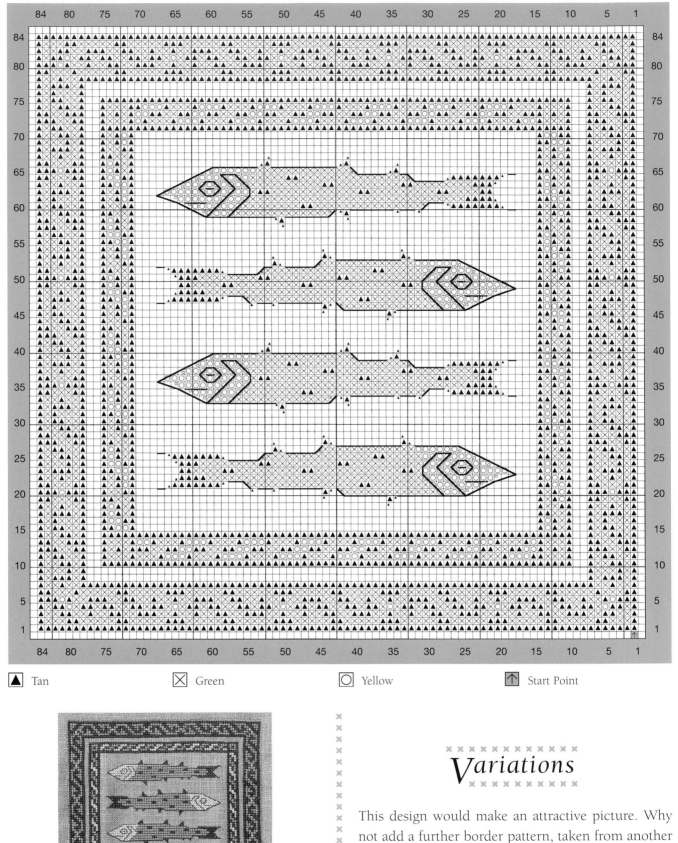

▲ Tan   ☒ Green   ◯ Yellow   ↑ Start Point

Variations

This design would make an attractive picture. Why not add a further border pattern, taken from another project in this book? Alternatively, just work the borders on Aida or canvas as a design for a mirror frame. Stretch the fabric around a strong mount and back with a mirror tile.

SWIMMING SALMON CUSHION

Although, according to legend, the salmon deserted Connla's Well, they were always regarded as sacred fish. Wells were also considered holy places of pilgrimage, for pagan and later Christian ceremonies of worship and healing.

Level ✱✱✱. The stitched design is 168 x 170 stitches, approximately 31 x 31.5 cm (12¼ x 12½ inches). Each stitch in this design is worked over TWO threads.

YOU WILL NEED:

✳ Fabric: 27 count evenweave fabric in turquoise, 50 x 120 cm (20 x 48 inches)
✳ Tapestry needle: size 26 and a sharp sewing needle
✳ Sewing thread: in turquoise to match fabric
✳ Cushion pad: 32 cm (12½ inches) square
✳ Thread: DMC 6-strand embroidery thread in the following colours and quantities:

Symbol	Colour	Shade	Skeins
▲	Tan	920	2
⊠	Green	907	1
⊡	Yellow	445	1

STITCHING INSTRUCTIONS

Preparation: Cut the fabric into three pieces: one piece 50 x 50 cm (20 x 20 inches) for the front, and two pieces 35 x 50 cm (14 x 20 inches) for the back. Oversew or bind the edges of the large square to prevent fraying while it is embroidered. Stitch the border, then plan the placement points of the salmon and mark each with a tacking thread before stitching.
Cross stitch: Use two strands of the embroidery thread and work each stitch over TWO blocks.
Backstitch: Use one strand of tan for the salmon details, except the tail tips which are worked with two strands of tan at the same time as the cross stitch.

Starting point: The charts overleaf show sections of the design: a corner, a length of the border and two fish swimming in opposite directions. Start at the point indicated by the arrow on the corner chart, which is 9 cm (3½ inches) from the right-hand side and 9 cm (3½ inches) from the bottom of the front square of fabric. Work this corner, then work a border of 29 cm (11½ inches) along the base of the cushion, and then the left-hand bottom corner. Continue the borders and corners to create a square. Cut five scraps of paper 2 x 10 cm (¾ x 4 inches) and using the photo for guidance, pin them on the cushion to mark the positions of the fish, which are worked last.

MAKING UP

Iron the embroidery on the back on a thick towel. It is best to use a sewing machine to make the cushion,

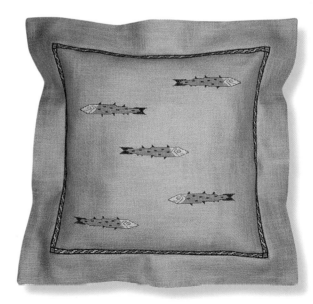

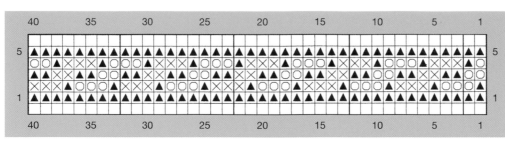

Section of border

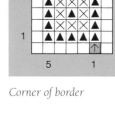

Corner of border

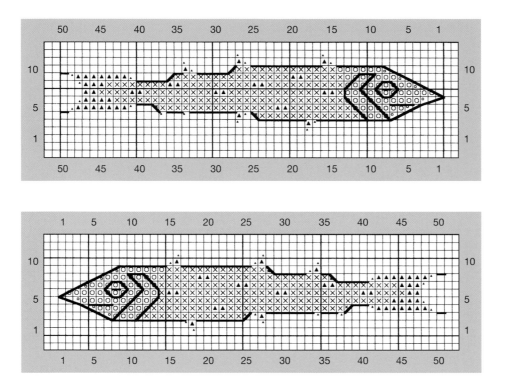

▲ Tan
✕ Green
○ Yellow
↑ Start Point

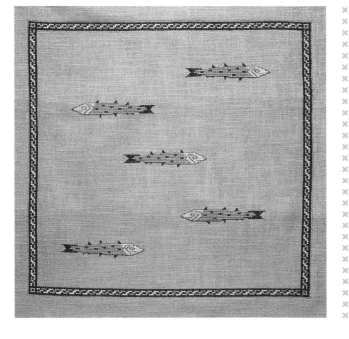

although it can be hand-sewn. Hem along one long side of each of the back pieces. Lay these pieces over the front, right sides together, with the hemmed edges overlapping at the centre back. Pin and tack the pieces together. With the wrong side of the embroidered front uppermost, draw a faint pencil square around the embroidery, 5 cm (2 inches) out from the embroidered border to create a square of about 41 x 41 cm (16 x 16 inches). Machine-stitch along the pencil lines. Remove tacking. Trim excess fabric back to 2 cm (1 inch) from this stitching. Mitre the corners. Turn right sides out and iron carefully on the back. Pin or tack through all layers to hold them together while machine-stitching around the cushion, as close as possible to the outside edge of the embroidered border. Insert the cushion pad.

SALMON
TISSUE SACHET

*When Finn had eaten the Salmon of
Knowledge, he had the power to see into the
future, by chanting a sacred poem and placing
his finger on the Tooth of Knowledge.*

Level ✱✱✱. The stitched design is 43 x 72 stitches, approximately 8 x 13 cm (3¼ x 5¼ inches). Each stitch in this design is worked over TWO threads.

YOU WILL NEED:

* Fabric: 27 count evenweave fabric in turquoise, 25 x 40 cm (10 x 16 inches)
* Tapestry needle: size 26 and a sharp sewing needle
* Sewing thread: in turquoise to match the fabric
* Packet of tissues
* Thread: DMC 6-strand embroidery thread in the following colours and quantities:

Symbol	Colour	Shade	Skeins
▲	Tan	920	1
☒	Green	907	1
◯	Yellow	445	1

STITCHING INSTRUCTIONS

Preparation: This sachet will hold a tissue pack measuring 5.5 x 11 cm (2¼ x 4¼ inches). If your pack is a different size, simply adjust the fabric sizes and the cross stitch border accordingly. Cut the fabric into three pieces: one piece measuring 18 x 25 cm (7 x 10 inches) for the front, and two pieces 11 x 25 cm (4½ x 10 inches) for the back. Oversew or bind the edges of the front piece of fabric so it does not fray while it is being embroidered.

Cross stitch: Use two strands of the embroidery thread and work each stitch over TWO threads.

Backstitch: Use one strand of tan for the salmon details, except the tail tips which are worked with two strands of tan at the same time as the cross stitch.

Starting point: This is indicated on the chart by an arrow. The first stitch should be made at a point 6 cm (2½ inches) from the right-hand side and 5 cm (2 inches) from the bottom of the front fabric square.

MAKING UP

Make up the tissue sachet in the same way as the Swimming Salmon cushion on page 19, except that the back pieces should be placed beside each other at the centre back rather than overlapping, and the edge of the rectangle is 1.5 cm (½ inch) from the embroidered border.

Variations

We love this turquoise fabric (called Meran) for its clear bright colour, but if you have difficulty obtaining it, any evenweave fabric in 27 or 28 count is suitable for this design and the others using Meran. Alternatively, you can work the sachet on 14 count Aida over one block per stitch. Both evenweaves and Aidas come in a wide range of colours which could be used for this project. Why not make sachets with golden fish on a cream background, tropical pinks on gold, or the graphic simplicity of black fish on white?

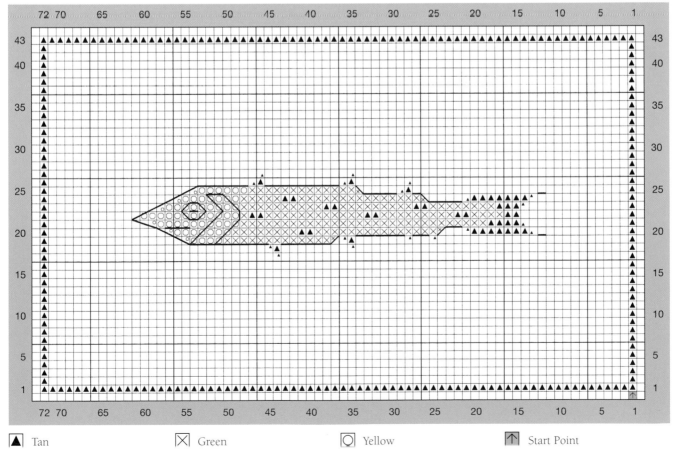

▲ Tan   ☒ Green   ⊙ Yellow   ↑ Start Point

WISE SALMON CARD AND GIFT TAG

Irish myths tell the story of a salmon that lived in a pool surrounded by the nine hazel trees of wisdom. In one magical hour, these trees would bloom and drop their fruit into the pool. The salmon ate the hazel nuts and became imbued with wisdom and healing gifts.

Level **✳✳**. The stitched card design is 23 x 62 stitches, approximately 9 x 3.25 cm (3½ x 1¼ inches). The stitched gift tag design is 15 x 54 stitches, approximately 2 x 7.75 cm (¾ x 3 inches).

YOU WILL NEED:

✳ Fabric: 2 pieces of 18 count Aida fabric in cream, 9 x 15 cm (3½ x 6 inches)
✳ Tapestry needle: size 26
✳ Card: in turquoise, cut to 15 x 20 cm (6 x 8 inches) for the card, and cut to 5 x 12 cm (2 x 5 inches) for the gift tag
✳ Narrow ribbon: 30 cm (12 inch) length in turquoise for the gift tag
✳ Stick glue or double-sided tape
✳ Thread: DMC 6-strand embroidery thread in the following colours and quantities:

Symbol	Colour	Shade	Skeins
▲	Tan	920	1
⊠	Green	907	1
⊙	Yellow	445	1

STITCHING INSTRUCTIONS

Cross stitch: Use two strands of the embroidery thread.
Backstitch: Use one strand of tan for the salmon details, except for the tail tips which are worked with two strands at the same time as the cross stitch. The backstitch border is also worked with two strands of tan. Work the complete chart for the card. For

the gift tag, work the inner backstitch border only.
Starting point: This is indicated on the chart by an arrow. The first stitch should be made at a point 4 cm (1½ inches) from the right-hand side and 4 cm (1½ inches) from the bottom of the fabric.

MAKING UP

Iron the embroidery on the back on a thick towel. The chart has a dotted line to indicate the cutting lines for the card (the cutting line for the gift tag is four blocks out from the backstitch border). Count out from the embroidery and carefully cut along the line of holes in the Aida. Fray back by one block, using the tip of a needle to tease out one thread at a time, pulling the threads away with the needle tip.
Card: Using a steel rule and craft knife, lightly score and fold the card to give a folded size of 10 x 15 cm (4 x 6 inches). Stick the embroidery onto the card using stick glue or double-sided tape.
Gift Tag: Make a hole near to one end of the card. Stick the embroidery towards the other end, using stick glue or double-sided tape. Thread the ribbon through the hole.

Variations

The colours of this salmon are taken from a page in the *Book of Kells*. Why not work the fish as a little silver trout, using a dark background fabric and silvery coloured threads?

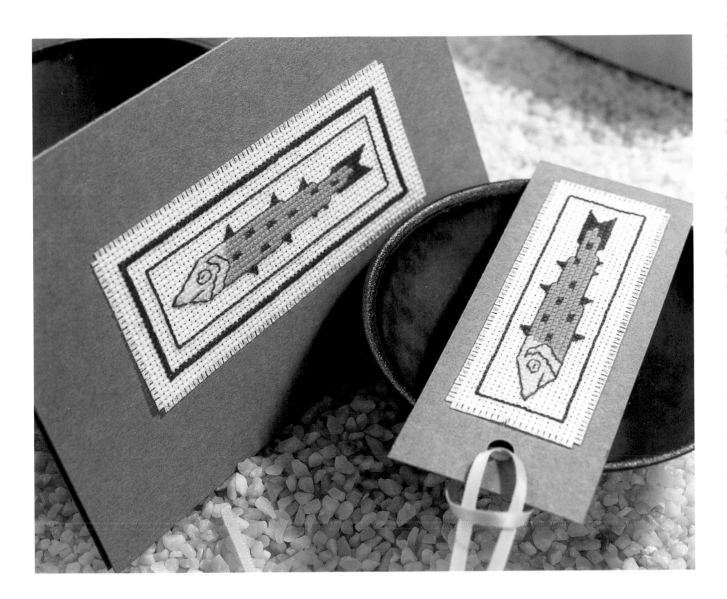

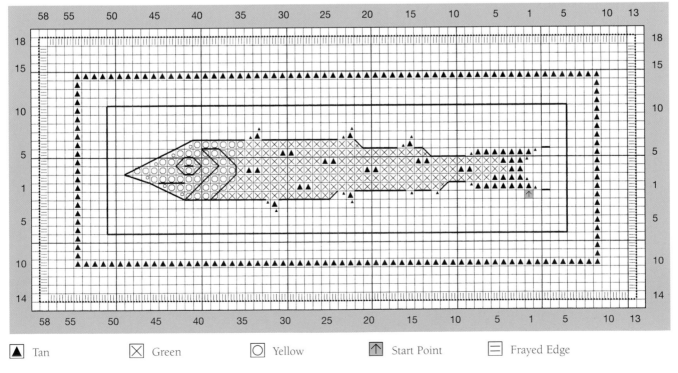

▲ Tan   ☒ Green   ○ Yellow   ↑ Start Point   ⊟ Frayed Edge

WATER JEWEL PURSE

Water was a sacred element for the Celts, providing a passage between the world of man and the underworld of the spirits. Offerings were made to these gods to persuade them to look kindly on men, and to invoke the healing powers of water. Jewels would be cast into the sea or wells as votive offerings.

Level ✶✶. The stitched design is 55 x 153 stitches, approximately 10 x 28 cm (4 x 11 inches).

YOU WILL NEED:

* Fabric: 14 count Aida fabric in cream, 16 x 34 cm (6½ x 13½ inches)
* Tapestry needle: size 24 and a sharp sewing needle
* Lining fabric: fine cotton in cream, 16 x 34 cm (6½ x 13½ inches)
* Beads: for trimming (optional)
* Velcro: a small piece or spot to fasten the purse
* Thread: DMC 6-strand embroidery thread in the following colours and quantities:

Symbol	Colour	Shade	Skeins
⊙	Pale Cream	712	1
◯	Dark Cream	739	1
✳	Dark Blue	791	1
◆	Mid Blue	825	1
△	Dark Green	3808	1
▲	Mid Green	3816	2

STITCHING INSTRUCTIONS

Cross stitch: Use three strands of the embroidery thread.

Starting point: This is indicated on the chart by an arrow. The first stitch should be made at a point 3 cm (1¼ inches) from the right-hand side and 3 cm (1¼ inches) from the bottom of the fabric. The shorter edges of the fabric are the top and bottom, the longer edges are the sides. The two front panels of the purse are shown overleaf as two separate charts. The back of the purse is worked with two outer vertical lines of 60 stitches in mid green. These are a continuation of the outer edges of the panel of vertical stripes (see diagram overleaf).

MAKING UP

Iron the embroidery on the back on a thick towel. Trim the edges of the fabric back to 2 cm (¾ inch) from the stitching. Fold over and iron the edges of the Aida one block out from the stitched edge. A single strand of pale cream is used to sew up the purse and lining. Mitre and trim the corners and stitch down neatly. Fold and iron the lining fabric to a shape just slightly smaller than the purse, trimming any excess fabric. Slipstitch the lining to the back of the purse. Fold and iron into a purse shape (see the photograph on the right), and overstitch the side seams together neatly and firmly. Sew the Velcro fastening, and the optional bead trimming, into place just beneath the purse flap.

Variations

Look at pictures of Celtic enamelware and metalwork for further inspiration. Work the purse with moody outline colours, studded with bright jewel-coloured lozenges of reds, greens and blues.

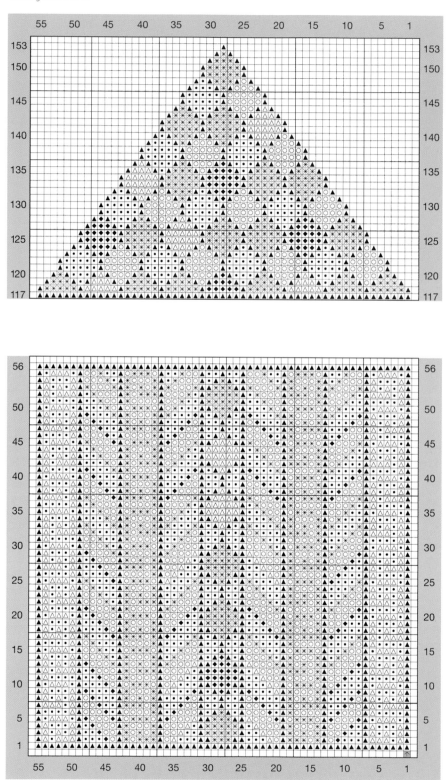

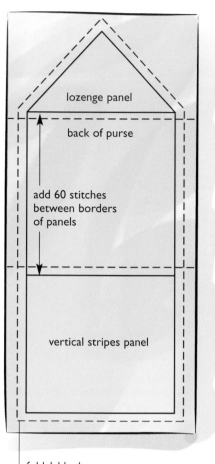

lozenge panel

back of purse

add 60 stitches
between borders
of panels

vertical stripes panel

fold 1 block
out from
embroidered
borders

- ● Pale Cream
- ○ Dark Cream
- ✳ Dark Blue
- ◆ Mid Blue
- △ Dark Green
- ▲ Mid Green
- ↑ Start Point

SEA SERPENT PURSE

The serpent was one of the most powerful of the Celtic deities. It was associated with wisdom and the renewal of life, echoing the ability of the snake to slough off its old skin. Its S-shape suggests running water, and the names for many rivers in Britain and Ireland are based on the local word for a snake. Sea serpents guarded the entry to the otherworld beneath the sea.

Level **✷✷**. The stitched design is 73 x 115 stitches, approximately 13.5 x 21 cm (5¼ x 8½ inches).

YOU WILL NEED:

✷ Fabric: 14 count Aida fabric in cream, 20 x 31 cm (8 x 12¼ inches)

✷ Tapestry needle: size 24 and a sharp sewing needle

✷ Lining fabric: fine cotton in cream, 20 x 31 cm (8 x 12¼ inches)

✷ Velcro: a small piece or spot to fasten the purse

✷ Thread: DMC 6-strand embroidery thread in the following colours and quantities:

Symbol	Colour	Shade	Skeins
⊠	Mid Green	3816	2
▲	Dark Green	3808	1
●	Pale Cream	712	1
⊞	Dark Cream	739	1
⊞	Dark Blue	781	1
◯	Mix (2 strands 3816 & 1 strand 3808)		

STITCHING INSTRUCTIONS

Cross stitch: Use three strands of the embroidery thread. Note that two different thread colours are worked together as a mix.

Backstitch: Use two strands of dark blue.

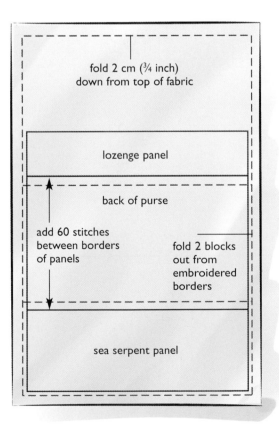

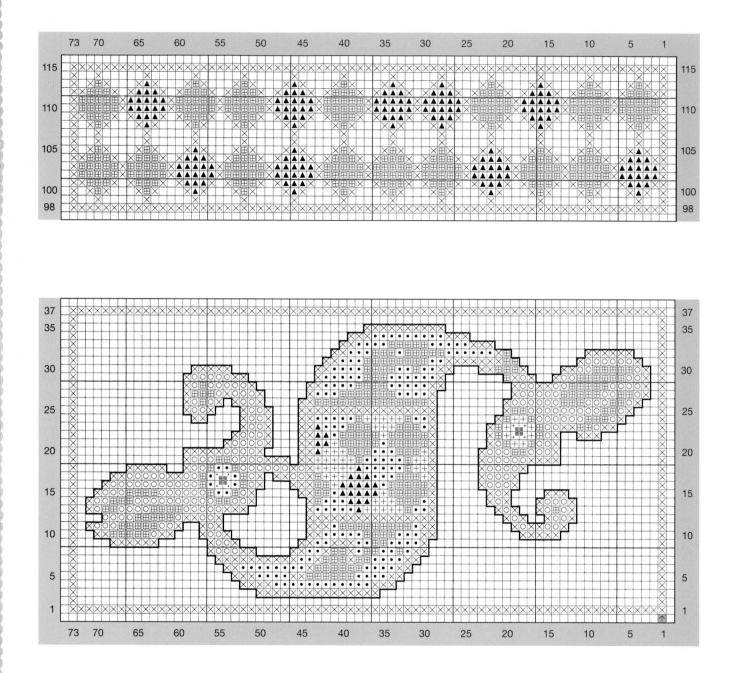

	Mid Green
▲	Dark Green
●	Pale Cream
＋	Dark Cream
⊞	Dark Blue
○	Mix (2 strands 3816 & 1 strand 3808)
↑	Start Point

Starting point: This is indicated on the chart by an arrow. The first stitch should be made at a point 3 cm (1¼ inches) in from the right-hand side and 3 cm (1¼ inches) from the bottom of the fabric. The shorter edges of the fabric are the top and bottom, the longer edges are the sides. The top and bottom front panels of the purse are shown as two separate charts. The back of the purse is worked with two outer vertical lines of 60 stitches of mid green between these panels, continuing the outer verticals of the front and back panels (see the diagram on page 29).

MAKING UP

Iron the embroidery on the back on a thick towel. Fold over and iron three sides of the Aida two blocks out from the stitched edge. Fold over and iron 2 cm (¾ inch) at the top edge. A single strand of pale cream thread is used to sew up the purse and lining. Mitre and trim the corners and stitch down neatly. Fold and iron the lining fabric to a shape slightly smaller than the purse. Slipstitch the lining to the back of the purse. Fold and iron into a purse shape (see photograph above), and overstitch the side seams together firmly. Neatly sew the Velcro fastening into place beneath the purse flap.

Variations

This purse was inspired by a dragon-shaped enamel brooch (see page 14). Why not work it in the glowing reds and browns of a fiery dragon?

FISH AND WAVE SAMPLER

Manannan Mac Lir, the Irish sea god, was the first king of the Isle of Man. His chariot was drawn by huge waves and he possessed a boat that obeyed his voice and a sword that could penetrate the thickest armour. Celtic Saints, such as Brendan, braved the dangers of the sea and its monsters, to bring Christianity to pagan tribes.

Level ✻. The stitched design is 74 x 80 stitches, approximately 14 x 14.5 cm (5½ x 5¾ inches).

YOU WILL NEED:

- Fabric: 14 count Aida fabric in cream, 25 x 25 cm (10 x 10 inches)
- Tapestry needles: sizes 24 & 26
- Card mount
- Masking tape
- Wadding (optional)
- Frame
- Thread: DMC 6-strand embroidery thread in the following colours and quantities:

Symbol	Colour	Shade	Skeins
☒	Pale Blue	747	1
✳	Dark Turquoise	992	1
△	Pale Turquoise	964	1
▲	Dark Blue	3765	2
◯	Lilac	3747	2
⊞	Mid Blue	519	1

STITCHING INSTRUCTIONS

Cross stitch: Use three strands of the embroidery thread and a size 24 tapestry needle.

Backstitch: Using a size 26 tapestry needle, use two strands of dark blue to work the fish tails and the flecks on the scales of the small fish. Use one strand of dark blue for the remaining backstitch. Some stitches are longstitches worked over two holes.

Starting point: This is indicated on the chart overleaf by an arrow. The first stitch should be made at a point 5 cm (2 inches) from the right-hand side and 5 cm (2 inches) from the top of the fabric.

MAKING UP

Iron the embroidery on the back on a thick towel. The dotted lines on the chart indicate the placement of the mount aperture. Measure this area carefully. Buy or make a mount to fit the size of your chosen frame. This sampler has an aperture size 14.3 cm x 14.3 cm (5¾ x 5¾ inches), and the overall size of the mount is 30 x 30 cm (12 x 12 inches). Centre the fabric carefully within the mount, trimming the Aida if necessary, and secure to the mount with masking tape. It is very effective to pad the embroidered area slightly. To do this, cut a piece of wadding slightly smaller than the aperture. Cut a piece of card the same size as the aperture. Place the wadding over the back of the embroidery, and the card on top of the wadding. Tape into place.

Variations

The motifs in this sampler are ideal for bathroom accessories. Use one or more of the borders as towel trims (see page 35), worked on either Aida band or a long strip of Aida fabric.

Use waste canvas to embroider a fish motif on a bathrobe or linen bag, decorate sweet-smelling sachets for soap or pot pourri with little fat fishes, or trim a roller blind with a wave motif.

	Pale Blue
	Dark Turquoise
	Pale Turquoise
	Dark Blue
	Lilac
	Mid Blue
	Start Point

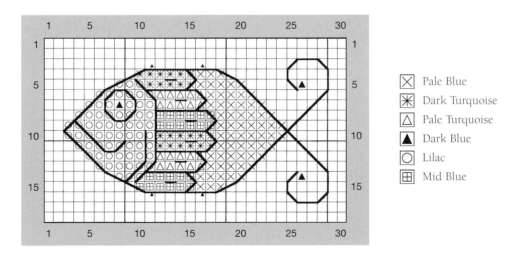

⊠	Pale Blue
✳	Dark Turquoise
△	Pale Turquoise
▲	Dark Blue
○	Lilac
⊞	Mid Blue

To make the fish towel trimming shown above, use 3.5 cm (1½ inch) wide Aida Band in white or cream. Work the Little Fish chart (above left) using the same embroidery threads and chart symbols as the sampler, but using two strands of thread for the cross stitch.

Each fish repeat is approximately 4.5 cm (1¾ inches) long. Work out the number of fish required for your towel width. You can adjust the number of empty blocks between each fish to space them evenly across the width of your towel.

RAINBOW FISH CARDS

Irish legend tells of the druid Finnegas, who found the salmon of knowledge, an enormous fish that had all the colours of the rainbow swirling and dancing on its gleaming skin. It was eaten by his pupil Finn, who gained wisdom and immense powers of magic.

Level ✱. These cards are worked on Aida fabric or Aida band in blue or tan colourways. The stitched design on the Aida fabric card is 44 x 48 stitches, approximately 6.25 x 6.75 cm (2½ x 2⅔ inches). The stitched design on the Aida band card is 22 x 36 stitches, approximately 3.75 cm x 6 cm (1½ x 2½ inches).

YOU WILL NEED:

* Fabric: 18 count Aida fabric in cream, 13 x 13 cm (5 x 5 inches) or 12 cm (5 inch) length of 5 cm (2 inch) wide Aida band in cream
* Tapestry needle: size 26
* Card: in turquoise, cut to 14 x 23 cm (5½ x 9 inches), and (to back Aida Band card only) 10 x 13 cm (4 x 5 inches)
* Steel rule and craft knife
* Stick glue or double-sided tape
* Thread: DMC 6-strand embroidery thread in alternative colours: blue or (in brackets) tan:

Symbol	Colour	Shade	Skeins
☒	Pale Blue (Dark Lime)	747 (704)	1
✴	Dark Turquoise (Pale Lime)	992 (3819)	1
△	Pale Turquoise	964 (3811)	1
▲	Dark Blue (Tan)	3765 (920)	1
⊙	Lilac (Pale Green)	3747 (3348)	1
⊞	Mid Blue (Dark Turquoise)	519 (597)	1

STITCHING INSTRUCTIONS

Cross stitch: Use two strands of embroidery thread.
Backstitch: Use two strands of dark blue (tan) for the fish tail. Use one strand of dark blue (tan) for the fish

details and for the side, outer and inner zigzag lines. Use two strands of dark turquoise for the centre zigzags of both colourways.

Starting point: This is indicated on the chart overleaf by an arrow. The first stitch of the Aida fabric card should be made at a point 4 cm (1½ inches) from the right-hand side and 6.5 cm (2½ inches) from the bottom of the fabric.

The first stitch of the Aida band card should be made at a point 3 cm (1¼ inches) from the right-hand side of the band and worked over the thirteenth block from the bottom of the band. The horizontal dotted lines, two squares above and below the fish, indicate the placement on the Aida band.

MAKING UP

Iron the embroidery on the back on a thick towel. Using a steel rule and a craft knife, lightly score and fold the card to give a folded size of 11.5 x 14 cm (4½ x 5½ inches).

Aida Fabric Card: The chart has an outer dotted line to indicate the fabric cutting lines. Count out from the embroidery and carefully cut along the lines of holes in the Aida. Fray back by two blocks, using the tip of a needle to tease out one thread at a time. Stick the embroidery centrally on the card using stick glue or double-sided tape.

Aida Band Card: On the inside front of the card, mark and cut two vertical slits 7.5 cm (3 inches) apart, and just wider than the Aida band. Slot the Aida band into these slits. Stick the ends of the Aida band to the inside of the card using stick glue or double-sided tape, cover with the backing card and stick down.

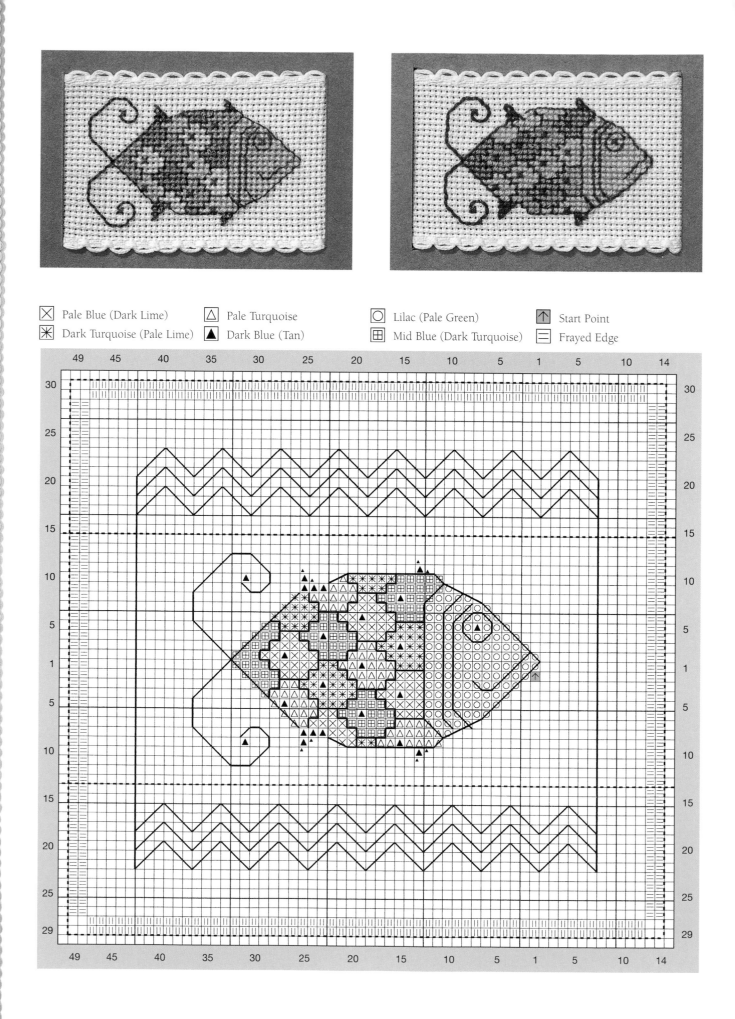

Pale Blue (Dark Lime) △ Pale Turquoise ○ Lilac (Pale Green) ↑ Start Point

✳ Dark Turquoise (Pale Lime) ▲ Dark Blue (Tan) ⊞ Mid Blue (Dark Turquoise) ═ Frayed Edge

Variations

Mount a rainbow fish in a frosted glass frame for a watery look. Our fish is worked on pale green Aida, with extra backstitch corner and border details in tan to complement the frame. Alternatively, make a gift tag by mounting the embroidery on a suitable piece of card and threading ribbons through a punched hole.

Intricate incisions on fine metalwork show the beautiful workmanship of the Celts.

FIRE

Fire was the element of heat and of the life-giving warmth of the sun, vital for the growth of crops. Fire kept man warm in the long, dark winter months. Fire melted the metal to be beaten into swords, shields and armour for protection in battle, and baked the clay fashioned into domestic pots and bowls. It was the element of destruction, of the flames that could burn down wooden houses, and of the dragon's breath that threatened the hero in his quest.

THE DESIGNS

The projects in this chapter reflect the linear characteristics of Celtic art. Sinuous shapes were incised into the clay or metal and filled in with finely detailed lines, with the decoration sometimes relying solely on the purity of these lines, or metal objects might be richly coloured with enamels. We have interpreted these lines either by simple, fine cross stitch shapes, or by an emphasis on backstitch. The use of

metal threads reflects their inspiration in Celtic metalwork. They add another dimension to cross stitch, and are worth the extra care that needs to be taken in stitching them. We have also shown how the scale of a design can be varied according to the choice of fabric – for example, a simple flame detail can be used as a small card when stitched on fine linen, or the complete shape can fill a cushion cover.

KNOT BOOKMARK

Pagan Celtic heroes did not die, but changed their shape to a different form and a new life. The knot was an expression of this idea of infinity. In many cultures it was taboo to imitate created life – the challenge for the artist was to use mathematics and geometry to create a line without either beginning or end, to symbolize this sense of endless continuity by interlacing borders and panels.

Level ✱. The stitched design is 19 x 107 stitches, approximately 3.5 x 17 cm (1¼ x 6¾ inches).

YOU WILL NEED:

* Fabric: 25 cm (10 inch) length of 5 cm (2 inch) wide Aida band in gold
* Tapestry needle: size 24 and a sharp sewing needle
* Narrow ribbon: 30 cm (12 inch) length in gold
* Felt: for backing in red, 4 x 17 cm (1½ x 6¾ inches)
* Thread: DMC 6-strand embroidery thread in the following colour and quantity:

Symbol	Colour	Shade	Skeins
☒	Red	815	1

STITCHING INSTRUCTIONS

Cross stitch: Use three strands of embroidery thread.
Starting point: This is indicated on the chart by an arrow. The first stitch should be made at a point 5 cm (2 inches) from the bottom of the Aida band and worked over the fifth block in from the right-hand side of the band.

MAKING UP

Iron the embroidery on the back on a thick towel. Fold over the ends one block out from the embroidered circle at the top and four blocks out from the embroidery at the bottom. Trim the folds to 2.5 cm (1 inch), turn in their sides and iron flat. Fold the ribbon in half and thread the loop end into a large-eyed needle. Tease open a hole in the fabric at the centre of the embroidered circle at the folded top of the bookmark. Attach the ribbon to the bookmark by pushing the needle and ribbon through and threading the ends of the ribbon through the loop. Pull taut. Sew the felt neatly on to the back of the bookmark.

Variations

By omitting the embroidered circle at the top of the design, it could be repeated with the narrow edges close to each other to decorate a towel border or curtain ties. The pattern could also be repeated with the long edges close to each other to make a square panel with an all-over design. Five repeats of the design (with two blocks left clear between each) will make a panel of 103 x 103 stitches, approximately 18 x 18 cm (7½ x 7½ inches) on 14 count fabric, to be used as the centre panel for a cushion. Try using a pale, cool shade on white Aida band, or bright, zingy citrus colours.

☒ Red
↑ Start Point
|| Aida band edge

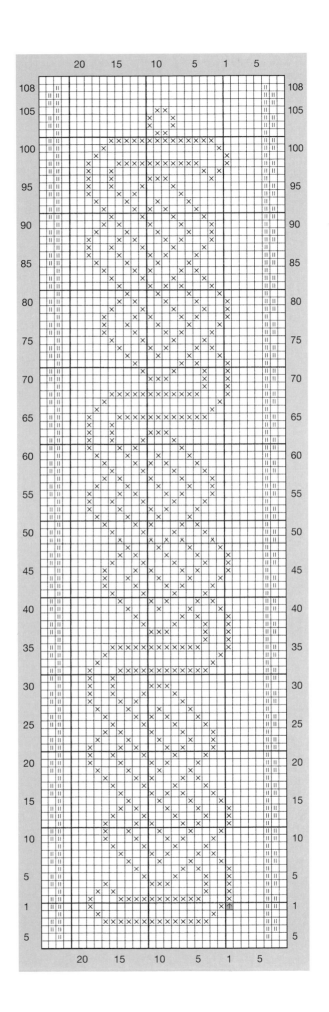

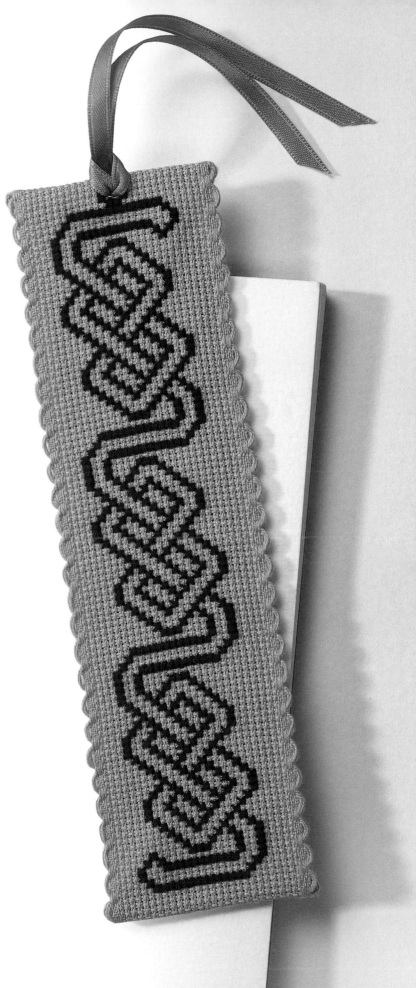

SERPENT AND KNOT KEYRINGS

There are close artistic links between Celtic art and that of the surrounding peoples – the Anglo-Saxons, the Picts and the Vikings. It is impossible to unravel these links, but certain characteristics stand out: images of dogs and hunting from the Anglo-Saxons, the incised sculptural lines of the Picts and here, the wide ribbon-like knots of the Norsemen.

Level **✱✱**. The stitched size of each design is 25 x 37 stitches, approximately 3.5 x 5 cm (1½ x 2 inches).

YOU WILL NEED:

✱ Fabric: 18 count Aida fabric in dark red, 8 x 11 cm (3 x 4½ inches) for each design
✱ Tapestry needle: size 26
✱ Rectangular key fobs: 5 x 6.5 cm (2 x 2¾ inches)
✱ Felt: for backing
✱ Threads: DMC 6-strand embroidery thread in the following colours and quantities:

Symbol	Colour	Shade	Skeins
Outline Knot Keyring			
⊠	Mid Gold	725	1
Serpent Knot Keyring			
▲	Dark Gold	832	1
◇	Blue	995	1
✳	Green	943	1
■	Black	310	1

Symbol	Colour	Shade	Skeins
Solid Knot Keyring			
▲	Dark Gold	832	1
⊠	Mid Gold	725	1
●	Pale Gold	727	1
◇	Blue	995	1
	Red	815	1

STITCHING INSTRUCTIONS

Cross stitch: Use one strand of embroidery thread.
Backstitch: *Serpent Knot keyring* only: use two strands of black.
Backstitch: *Solid Knot keyring* only: use two strands of red.
Starting point: This is indicated on all three charts by an arrow towards the bottom right-hand corner. With the long edges of the fabric vertical, the first stitch should be made at a point 2.5 cm (1 inch) from the right-hand side and 2.5 cm (1 inch) from the bottom of the fabric.

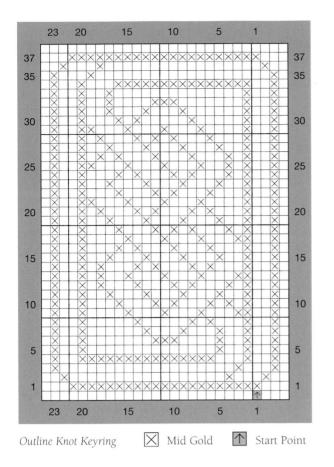

Outline Knot Keyring ☒ Mid Gold ⬆ Start Point

MAKING UP

Iron the embroidery on the back on a thick towel. Make sure that the inside of the key fob is clean, then cut the fabric one block out from the embroidered border, or to fit your key fob. It is best not to cut the fabric before you are ready to put it into the fob as the Aida frays easily. Cut a piece of felt to the same size as the cut Aida to cover the back of the stitching. Place the two pieces in the fob and close.

Variations

Use thread colours to match your kitchen and fit the embroidery into ready-made fridge magnets. Use the designs as gift tags mounted on thin card with a matching ribbon added. Stitch one of the designs on a larger scale fabric to make up into a greetings card.

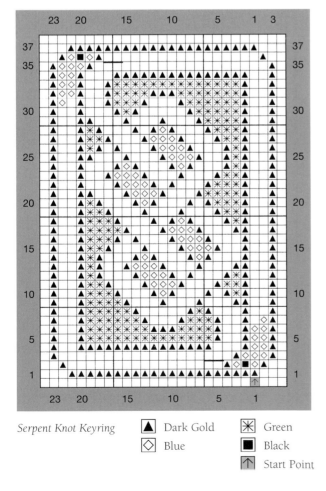

Serpent Knot Keyring
▲ Dark Gold ✳ Green
◇ Blue ■ Black
⬆ Start Point

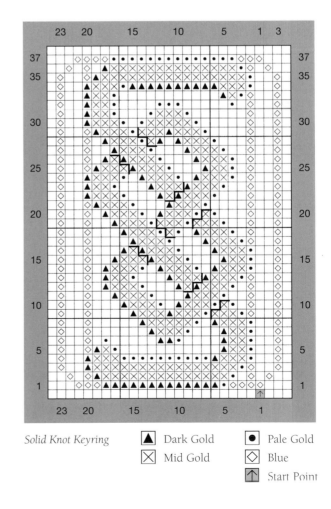

Solid Knot Keyring
▲ Dark Gold ● Pale Gold
☒ Mid Gold ◇ Blue
⬆ Start Point

INCISED WARE BOOK COVER

The majority of Celtic art is found on portable, practical objects. The remains of drinking vessels, with simple decoration incised on the earthenware before firing, have been found in the graves and tombs of wealthy noblemen. At times when burial rites included cremation, only fragments survived inside pottery urns, themselves decorated with incised patterns.

Level **✳✳✳**. The stitched design is 75 x 75 stitches, approximately 13.5 x 13.5 cm (5¼ x 5¼ inches). Each stitch in this design is worked over TWO threads. The matching bookmark instructions are given on page 49.

YOU WILL NEED:

✳ Spiral-bound book
✳ Fabric: 28 count evenweave fabric in pale grey. The amount of fabric needed depends on the size of the book (see below).
✳ Tacking thread
✳ Scrap paper
✳ Tapestry needle: size 26 and a sharp sewing needle
✳ Sewing thread: in pale grey, to match evenweave fabric
✳ Thread: DMC 6-strand embroidery thread in the following colours and quantities:

Symbol	Colour	Shade	Skeins
✳	Metallic Copper	5279	1
	Dark Blue	924	1

AMOUNT OF FABRIC NEEDED

To work out how much fabric you will need, measure the width of the front cover of the spiral bound book, including the spiral. Multiply this by 3½ to give the width of fabric needed. Measure the height of the book, and add 4 cm (1½ inches) to give the height of fabric needed (see diagram overleaf).

STITCHING INSTRUCTIONS

Each stitch in this design is worked over TWO threads.

Cross stitch: Use one strand of metallic copper.
Backstitch: Use one strand of metallic copper to work the outlines of the rectangles and two strands of dark blue embroidery thread for the infill pattern.
Starting point: This is indicated on the chart overleaf by an arrow. To find the position of the first stitch, tack along the lines shown on the diagram, using your spiral book measurements. Tack diagonal lines on the front section. Cut a piece of thin scrap paper into a 6 cm (2¼ inch) square. On the right side of the evenweave, centre the paper on the diagonal and pin in place as a guide for the first stitch, which should be made at the bottom right-hand corner. Remove the paper before stitching.

MAKING UP

Iron the embroidery on the back on a thick towel. Sew a single hem on each of the short edges. Fold right sides together at each end and pin. Leave a seam allowance of 1.5 cm (½ inch) and sew at top and bottom to make pockets for the covers of the book. Turn right sides out. Iron on the back, ironing a fold at the top and bottom of the spine section. Slip the cover on to the back and front covers of the book.

Variations

The book could be used as a visitors book, a daily journal, a photograph album, or a memento book for recording special occasions. Add a date or initials to the cover if you wish.

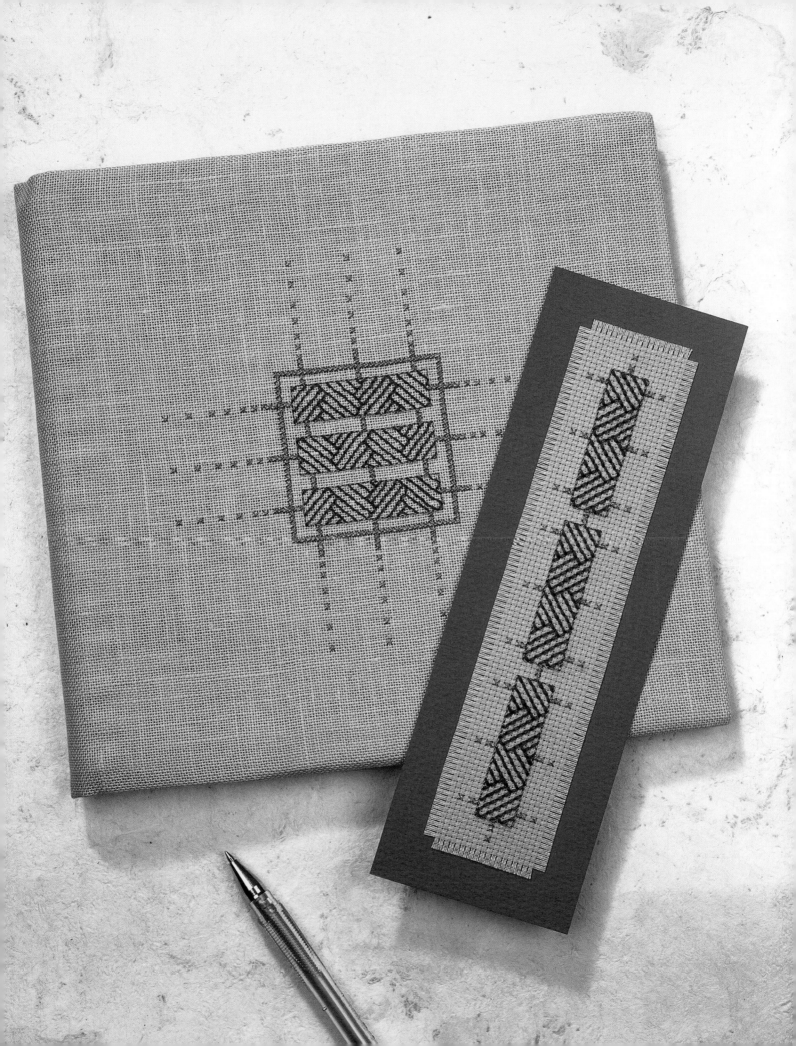

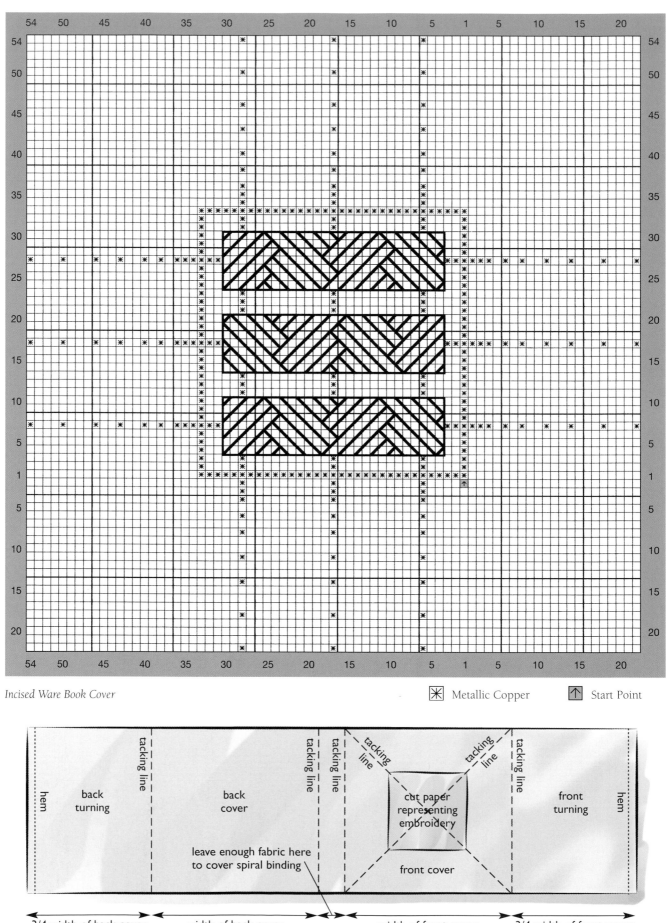

Incised Ware Book Cover

✳ Metallic Copper   ↑ Start Point

| hem | back turning | back cover | tacking line | tacking line | cut paper representing embroidery | front cover | tacking line | front turning | hem |

leave enough fabric here
to cover spiral binding

← 3/4 width of back cover → ← width of back cover → ← width of front cover → ← 3/4 width of front cover →

INCISED WARE BOOKMARK

Warriors and druids had great status in early Celtic life. The druid class seems to have included not just priests, but bards and craftsmen. Metalwork was a highly regarded craft, as beautiful armour was a sign of warrior status. Shields and swords were decorated with incised or raised designs, and sometimes embellished with enamelwork and jewels.

Level ✱✱. The stitched design is 15 x 95 stitches, approximately 3 x 17.5 cm (1¼ x 6¾ inches). See page 47 for a photograph of the finished item.

YOU WILL NEED:

* Fabric: 14 count Aida fabric in pale grey, 10 x 25 cm (4 x 10 inches)
* Tapestry needle: size 24
* Card: in blue, 7 x 22 cm (2¾ x 8¾ inches)
* Stick glue or double-sided tape
* Thread: DMC 6-strand embroidery thread in the following colours and quantities:

Symbol	Colour	Shade	Skeins
✳	Metallic Copper	5279	1
	Dark Blue	924	1

STITCHING INSTRUCTIONS

Cross stitch: Use one strand of metallic copper.
Backstitch: Use one strand of metallic copper and three strands of dark blue.
Starting point: Start by working the outlines of the rectangles using one strand of metallic copper. The position of the first backstitch is indicated on the chart by an arrow. With the long edges of the fabric horizontal, the first backstitch should be made at a point 4 cm (1½ inches) from the bottom and 4 cm (1½ inches) from the left-hand edge of the fabric.

MAKING UP

Iron the embroidery on the back on a thick towel. The chart has a dotted line to indicate the cutting lines. Count out from the embroidery and carefully cut along the lines of the holes in the Aida. Fray back by two blocks, using the tip of a needle to tease out one thread at a time. Stick the embroidery centrally on the card using stick glue or double-sided tape.

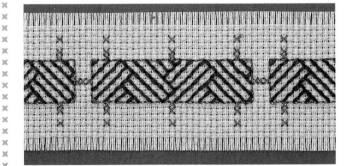

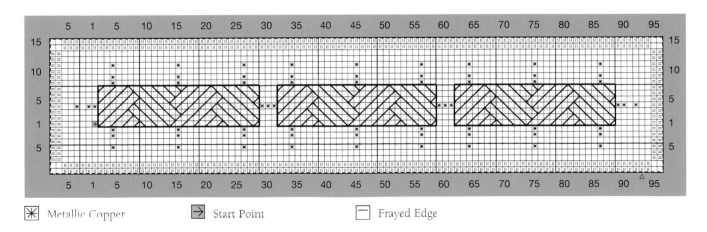

✳ Metallic Copper	➔ Start Point	⊟ Frayed Edge

SUN CUSHIONS

Fire festivals were used to mark important changes in the seasons. For Celts living in the north, the growing strength of the sun as winter changed to summer was of enormous significance. Beltane, named after Belanus, the god of fire, was celebrated on 1st May, marking the beginning of summer and the pasturing of cattle in the fields. Druids guided the ceremonies where fires were lit on hilltops and cattle driven between gates of fire. Lughnasadh was the festival of late summer and the harvest. It was named after Lugh, the god of the sun, whose heat had made the crops grow. Lugh was a formidable warrior and magician. Metalwork was an important Celtic art, and legend tells of Lugh using his power over fire to forge weapons to help Cu Chulainn in his battles.

The Beltane Sun Cushion is shown on the left, the Lugh Sun Cushion on the right.

Level ✱✱. The stitched designs are each 87 x 87 stitches. The Beltane design measures approximately 14 x 14 cm (5½ x 5½ inches); Lugh measures approximately 28 x 28 cm (11 x 11 inches). Both cushions use the same chart.

YOU WILL NEED:

For the Beltane Sun Cushion

✱ Fabric: 16 count Aida fabric in dark grey, 38 x 38 cm (15 x 15 inches)
✱ Tapestry needle: size 26 and a sharp sewing needle
✱ Thread: DMC 6-strand embroidery thread in the following colours and quantities:

Symbol	Colour	Shade	Skeins
⊠	Red	815	1
◼	Metallic Grey	5287	1

For the Lugh Sun Cushion

✱ Fabric: 16 count Aida fabric in pale grey, 38 x 38 cm (15 x 15 inches)
✱ Tapestry needle: size 24 and a sharp sewing needle
✱ Thread: DMC 6-strand embroidery thread in the following colours and quantities:

Symbol	Colour	Shade	Skeins
⊠	Dark Blue	924	2
◼	Metallic Copper	5279	1

For both Cushions

✱ Border and backing fabric: silk fabric in a matching shade of grey, 33 x 70 cm (13 x 26 inches)
✱ Sewing thread: to match border and backing fabric
✱ Cushion pad: 30 cm (12 inches) square

STITCHING INSTRUCTIONS

For the Beltane Sun Cushion

Cross stitch: Use two strands of red and one strand of metallic grey. Each stitch in this design is worked over ONE block.

For the Lugh Sun Cushion

Cross stitch: Use three strands of blue and two strands of metallic copper. Each stitch in this design is worked over TWO blocks.

Starting point for Beltane cushion: This is indicated on the chart overleaf by an arrow. The first stitch should be made at a point 16.5 cm (6½ inches) from the right-hand side of the fabric and 18 cm (7 inches) from the bottom of the fabric.

Starting point for Lugh cushion: This is indicated on the chart overleaf by an arrow. The first stitch should be made at a point 15 cm (6 inches) from the right-hand side of the fabric and 16.5 cm (6½ inches) from the bottom of the fabric.

MAKING UP

For both Beltane and Lugh Sun Cushions

It is best to use a sewing machine to make up the cushion. Cut the silk fabric into four strips 6 x 33 cm (2 x 13 inches) for the front borders and two pieces 23 x 33 cm (9 x 13 inches) for the back. Hem one long edge on each of the back pieces.

Iron the embroidery on the back on a thick towel. Fold the four border strips in half with long edges together and iron the folds. For the Beltane cushion, on the embroidered Aida fabric measure out 9.5 cm (3¾ inches) from the outermost stitches and draw light lines at these measurements using a soft pencil. For the Lugh cushion, measure out 2.5 cm (1 inch) and draw light lines. This should give you a square of 33 cm (13 inches). Cut the Aida fabric along these lines. With right sides together and raw edges to the

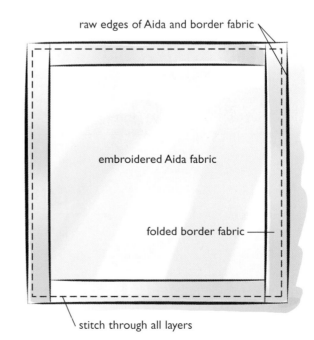

raw edges of Aida and border fabric

embroidered Aida fabric

folded border fabric

stitch through all layers

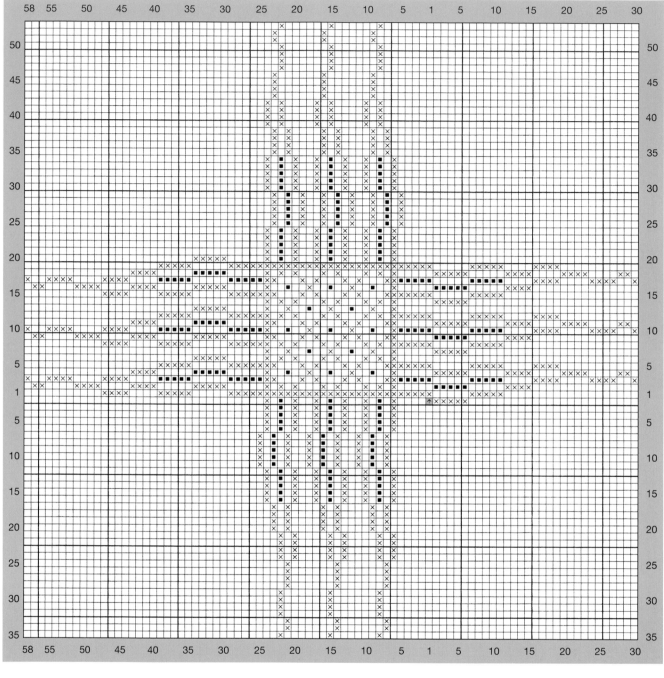

outside, pin a folded border strip to each edge of the Aida. Tack through all the layers close to the raw edges (see diagram on page 51).

Lay the two back pieces over the embroidered front, right sides together, with the hemmed edges overlapping at the centre. Tack in place. Sew all round leaving a 1.5 cm (½ inch) seam allowance. Turn right sides out. Iron on the back, then insert the cushion pad.

↑ Start Point

Beltane Sun Cushion
☒ Red
■ Metallic Grey

Lugh Sun Cushion
☒ Dark Blue
■ Metallic Copper

FIRE CARD

An Irish legend tells of a druid, Midhe, who brought the gift of fire to Ireland. He lit a fire upon a hill, where it burned for seven years. All the fires in Ireland were lit from this fire, but the local druids were jealous of his power and debated how to challenge his authority. Midhe's response was to cut out their tongues and bury them under the hill of Uaisnech.

Level ✱✱✱. The stitched design is 34 x 35 stitches, approximately 3 x 3 cm (1¼ x 1¼ inches). Each stitch in this design is worked over ONE thread.

YOU WILL NEED:

* Fabric: 28 count evenweave in pale grey, 9 x 9 cm (3½ x 3½ inches)
* Tapestry needle: size 26
* Card: in red, cut to 9 x 18 cm (3½ x 7 inches)
* Steel rule and craft knife
* Stick glue or double-sided tape
* Thread: DMC 6-strand embroidery thread in the following colours and quantities:

Symbol	Colour	Shade	Skeins
▲	Red	815	1
◯	Dark Blue	924	1

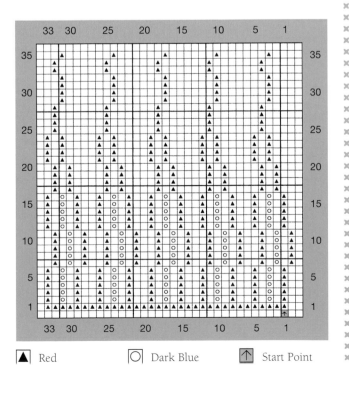

▲ Red   ◯ Dark Blue   ↑ Start Point

STITCHING INSTRUCTIONS

Each stitch in this design is worked over ONE thread.
Cross stitch: Use one strand of embroidery thread.
Starting point: This is indicated on the chart by an arrow. The first stitch should be made at a point 3 cm (1¼ inches) from the right-hand side and 3 cm (1¼ inches) from the bottom of the fabric.

MAKING UP

Iron the embroidery on the back on a thick towel. The cutting line is approximately 11 threads from the edge of the embroidery. Count out from the embroidery and carefully cut along the lines of the holes in the evenweave fabric. Fray back by three threads, gently using the tip of a needle to tease out just one thread at a time. Using a steel rule and a craft knife, lightly score and then fold the card to give a folded size of 9 x 9 cm (3½ x 3½ inches). Carefully stick the embroidery centrally on the card using either stick glue or double-sided tape.

DRAGON SPECTACLE CASE

Tales from ancient Brittany speak of a dangerous demon, a dragon terrifying the people. Arthur of Britain was summoned to slay it but after three days and nights of battle, it was finally Efflam, the son of the King of Ireland, who lured the monster to its death by the sea.

Level ✳✳. The stitched design is 42 x 84 stitches, approximately 7.5 x 15 cm (3 x 6 inches).

YOU WILL NEED:

✳ Fabric: 14 count Aida fabric in pale grey, 23 x 23 cm (9 x 9 inches)

✳ Tapestry needle: size 24 and a sharp sewing needle

✳ Sewing thread in pale grey to match Aida fabric, in bright blue to match cord, and in red to match felt

✳ Cord: 40 cm (16 inch) length of bright blue cord

✳ Lining fabric: piece of red felt, 20 x 20 cm (8 x 8 inches)

✳ Thread: DMC 6-strand embroidery thread in the following colours and quantities:

Symbol	Colour	Shade	Skeins
▲	Red	815	1
◯	Dark Blue	924	1
◆	Bright Blue	995	1
⬤	Green	943	1
✳	Metallic Copper	5279	1

STITCHING INSTRUCTIONS

Cross stitch: Use three strands of embroidery thread and one strand of the metallic thread.

Backstitch: Use three strands of dark blue and one strand of metallic copper.

Starting point: This is indicated on the chart by an arrow. The first stitch should be made at a point 3 cm (1¼ inches) from the left-hand side and 3 cm (1¼ inches) from the top of the fabric.

MAKING UP

Iron the embroidery on the back on a thick towel. Fold right sides together along a line two blocks out from the right hand edge of the embroidered border. Sew along the base and side of the case using small backstitches, two blocks out from the outermost edges of the embroidered border, and leaving a small gap at the bottom folded corner for the cord. Trim, mitre the corners slightly and turn right sides out. Fold in the top, two blocks up from the border. Insert the cord in the gap. Catch-stitch the cord to the base and side of the case, ending in a loop at the top. Stitch the other end of the cord securely to the inside top of the case. Make a pocket of felt to fit inside the case. Insert the felt and stitch the felt neatly around the inside top edge of the case.

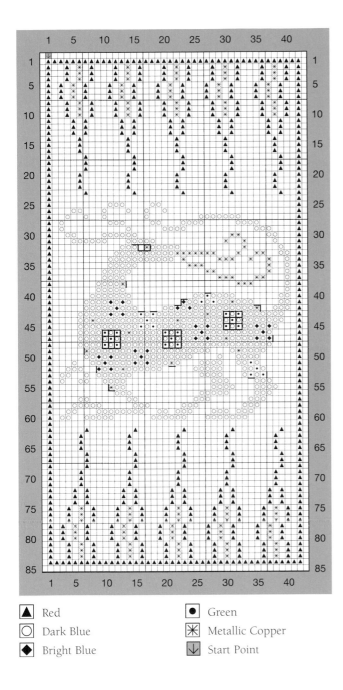

■ Red   ● Green

○ Dark Blue   ✳ Metallic Copper

◆ Bright Blue   ↓ Start Point

DRAGON CARD

Level ✱✱✱. The stitched design is 38 x 36 stitches, approximately 3.5 x 3.5 cm (1½ x 1½ inches).

YOU WILL NEED:

✳ Fabric: 28 count evenweave in pale grey, size 9 x 9 cm (3½ x 3½ inches)

✳ Tapestry needle: size 26

✳ Card: in red, 9 x 18 cm (3½ x 7 inches)

✳ Stick glue or double-sided tape

✳ Thread: DMC 6-strand embroidery thread in the following colours and quantities:

Symbol	Colour	Shade	Skeins
■	Red	815	1
○	Dark Blue	924	1

STITCHING INSTRUCTIONS

Each stitch in this design is worked over ONE thread.
Cross stitch: Use one strand of embroidery thread.
Starting point: This is shown on the chart by an arrow. The first stitch is 3 cm (1¼ inches) from the right-hand side and 3 cm (1¼ inches) from the bottom. See page 53 for making up instructions.

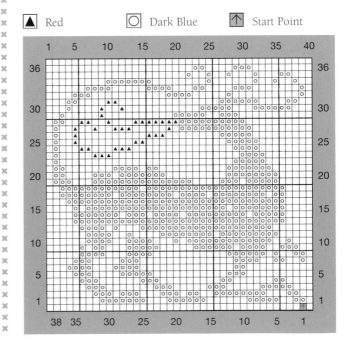

■ Red   ○ Dark Blue   ↑ Start Point

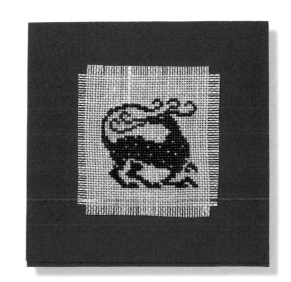

This Evangelist, from the Book of Durrow, *has a wonderful naïve simplicity.*

IR

Air was one of the divine elements. It embraced the flight of angels and birds and was the element of the sun, moon and stars. Christ and the evangelists were enthroned in glory in the heavens. Mysterious three-armed whirligigs spun through space, protecting men from evil spirits. In the same way that clouds change their shape, Celtic deities could change from human form to bird and back again.

THE DESIGNS

In this chapter you will find a wide variety of practical projects for different activities and rooms in the home. There are sewing accessories, items for the desktop and the dressing table, and also for the wardrobe. They all draw on the rich motifs of Celtic illuminated manuscripts, some of them inspired by the original colours and others worked using more contemporary colours. When you have worked some of the projects in this chapter, why not try some of the projects in your own choice of colours, inspired by these wonderful old manuscripts? There are many books available illustrating these gospels and they are a pleasure to pore over.

CELTIC ANGEL PINCUSHION

*Pagan Celts considered it profane to depict their gods in human form.
As a result, there was no artistic tradition to portray holy Christian
figures. Saints and angels were illustrated in stiff poses strongly
influenced by the Byzantine art of the early Christian church. Angels
were regarded as mediators between men and God.*

Level ✱. The stitched design is 40 x 40 stitches, approximately 9 x 9 cm (3½ x 3½ inches).

YOU WILL NEED:

✱ Fabric: 11 count Aida fabric in pale blue, 15 x 15 cm (6 x 6 inches)
✱ Tapestry needle: size 22 and a sharp sewing needle
✱ Backing fabric: Use either a co-ordinating cotton fabric or a second piece of pale blue Aida, 15 x 15 cm (6 x 6 inches)
✱ Stuffing
✱ Cord: 55 cm (22 inch) length of gold cord for trimming (optional)
✱ Thread: DMC 6-strand embroidery thread and DMC metallic thread in the following colours and quantities:

Symbol	Colour	Shade	Skeins
⊠	Dark Gold	832	1
✳	Dark Blue	930	1
▲	Mid Blue	793	1
◇	Pale Blue	341	1
●	Very Pale Blue	3753	1
⊙	Metallic Gold	5282	1

STITCHING INSTRUCTIONS

Cross stitch: Use four strands of the embroidery thread and two strands of the metallic thread. Cut the embroidery threads in multiples of two lengths, and divide into three sets of four strands.

Backstitch and long stitch: Use one strand of dark blue for all the backstitch, except the stars on the cloak which are worked using two strands of metallic gold.

Starting Point: This is indicated on the chart by an arrow. The first stitch should be made at a point 3 cm (1¼ inches) from the right hand side and 3 cm (1¼ inches) from the bottom of the fabric.

MAKING UP

Iron the embroidery and the backing fabric on the back on a thick towel. Place right sides together and pin and tack together. Use a single strand of pale blue to sew around the pincushion using small backstitches, two blocks out from the outer border, leaving a gap of 5 cm (2 inches) along the base. Trim excess fabric and mitre the corners. Turn right sides out and iron gently on the back. Stuff firmly and sew up the gap. If using the cord trimming, leave a small space in this gap to insert the cord ends. Insert one end of the cord into the gap, and using a single strand of dark gold, sew the cord around the edge of the pincushion over the seam. At each corner, twist the cord into a small loop, sew down securely and continue. Cut off any excess cord, push the cord end through the same gap and sew down.

Variations

Use this design for a matching needlecase, following the format of the Celtic Swan needlecase on page 69, but using 11 count Aida.

Work the design on 14 or 18 count Aida fabric in dark, rich colours, and mount in an aperture card with a gold frame. Add to your collection of angels and icons.

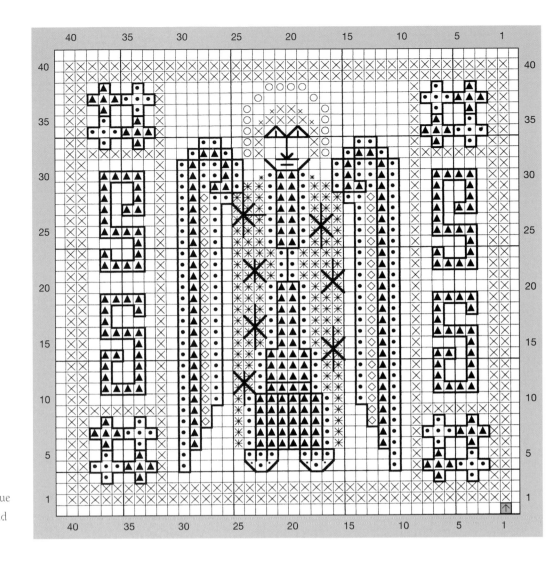

- ⊠ Dark Gold
- ✳ Dark Blue
- ▲ Mid Blue
- ◇ Pale Blue
- ● Very Pale Blue
- ○ Metallic Gold
- ↑ Start Point

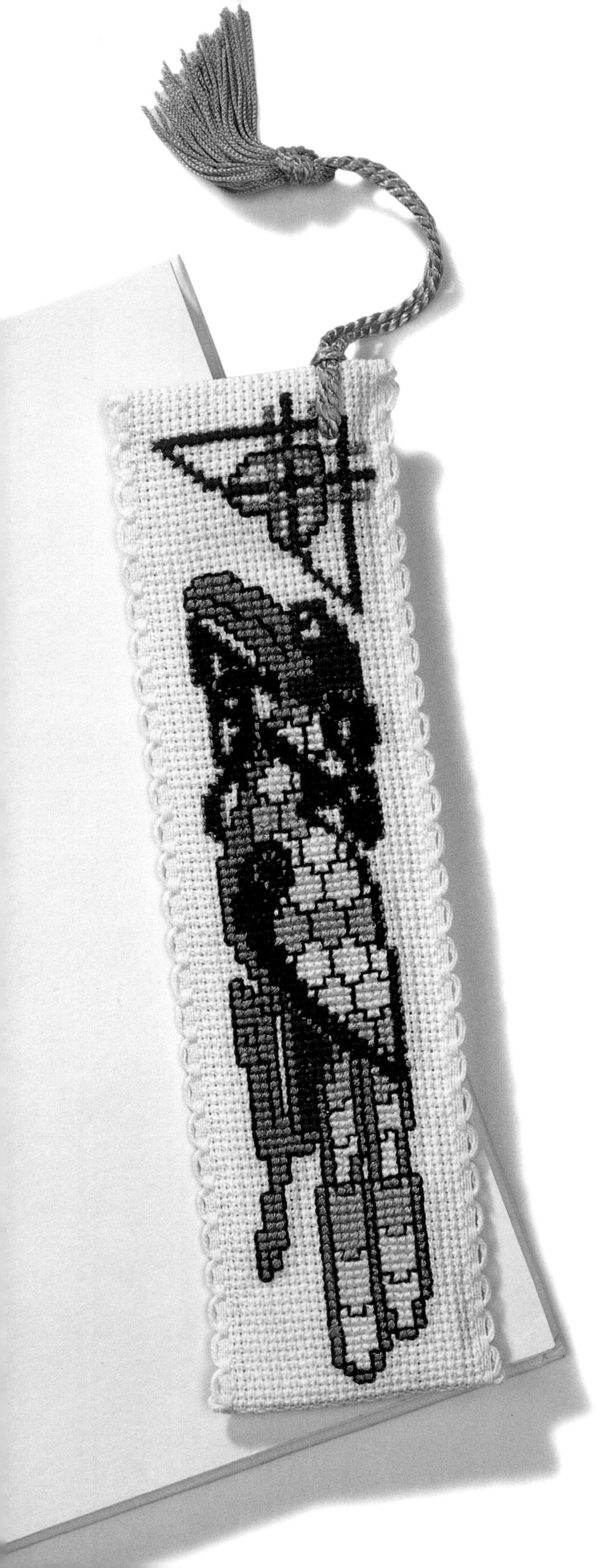

EAGLE BOOKMARK

In a cycle of Welsh legends, King Arthur helped his cousin Culhwch perform a series of tasks in order to win the hand of Olwen, the daughter of a giant. They were helped by an eagle and his friend, the salmon, who carried them along the river to the town of Gloucester. There is still an eagle to be found there today, incised into a stone by a spring.

Level ✳✳. The stitched design is 24 x 105 stitches, approximately 4 x 17.5 cm (1½ x 7 inches).

YOU WILL NEED:

✳ Fabric: 25 cm (10 inches) of 5 cm (2 inch) wide Aida Band in cream
✳ Tapestry needle: size 24 and a sharp sewing needle
✳ Thin white card: for stiffening (optional)
✳ Tassel or ribbon: for trimming
✳ Ribbon or fabric: for backing
✳ Thread: DMC 6-strand embroidery thread in the following colours and quantities:

Symbol	Colour	Shade	Skeins
⊠	Dark Gold	832	1
⊞	Mid Gold	834	1
◇	Pale Gold	745	1
✳	Dark Blue	336	1
△	Mid Blue	796	1
⊞	Cream	746	1

STITCHING INSTRUCTIONS

Cross stitch: Use three strands of the embroidery thread.

Backstitch: Use two strands of dark gold to outline and work details on the dark blue areas, and two strands of dark blue for the remaining backstitch.

Starting point: This is indicated on the chart by an arrow. The first stitch is worked over the fifth block from the right scalloped edge and 5 cm (2 inches) from the bottom of the fabric.

MAKING UP

Iron the embroidery on the back on a thick towel. Fold over the ends of the bookmark three blocks out from the top and bottom stitches. Trim these folds to 2.5 cm (1 inch) and turn in their sides. Attach a tassel or a ribbon at the point indicated by a dot on the chart, and knot into place. Cut a piece of thin white card slightly shorter and narrower than the finished bookmark. Fold and iron the backing ribbon or fabric to the correct size, and slipstitch to the back of the bookmark, slipping the card between the backing and the bookmark as you sew.

Variations

Why not take this design further to make a set of desk accessories? The eagle design could be used on a piece of 14 count Aida to decorate a matching book cover, and two or more eagles worked on a long strip of fabric could be used to edge a padded desk mat to protect a tabletop from your computer. Work the set in colourways to match the decor of your room.

⊠	Dark Gold	△	Mid Blue
⊞	Mid Gold	⊞	Cream
◇	Pale Gold	↑	Start Point
✳	Dark Blue	‖	Aida Band Edge

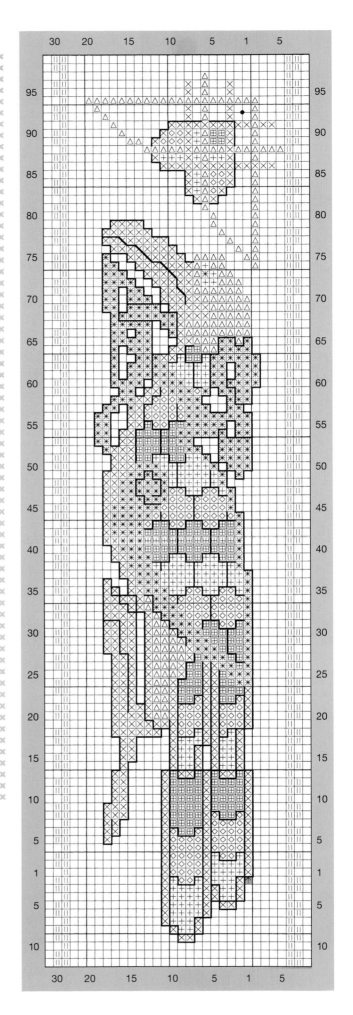

EAGLE BOX

Many Celtic bird designs portray an eagle and were obviously influenced by Jupiter, the Roman god of the skies, whose symbol was an eagle and whose sacred tree was the oak. In one Welsh legend, the warrior Lleu was mortally injured, but turned into an eagle and flew to an oak tree to escape death.

Level ✳. The stitched design is 26 x 39 stitches, approximately 3.5 x 5.5 cm (1¾ x 2¼ inches).

YOU WILL NEED:

✳ Fabric: 18 count Aida fabric in cream, 8 x 10 cm (3 x 4 inches)
✳ Tapestry needle: size 26
✳ Small box
✳ Stick glue or double-sided tape

✳ Thread: DMC 6-strand embroidery thread in the following colours and quantities:

Symbol	Colour	Shade	Skeins
☒	Dark Gold	832	1
⊞	Mid Gold	834	1
⊙	Pale Gold	745	1
◯	Cream	746	1
△	Blue	796	1

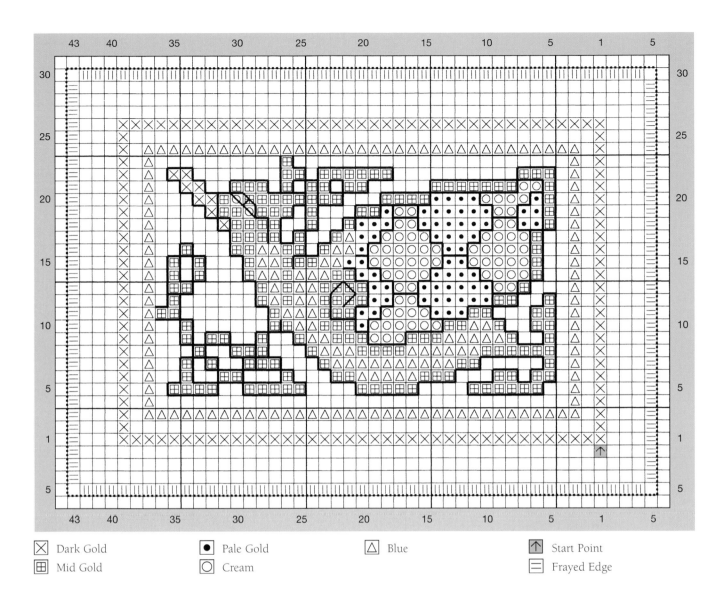

☒	Dark Gold	●	Pale Gold	

☒ Dark Gold　　● Pale Gold　　△ Blue　　⬆ Start Point

⊞ Mid Gold　　○ Cream　　　　　　　　　　⊟ Frayed Edge

STITCHING INSTRUCTIONS

Cross stitch: Use two strands of embroidery thread .
Backstitch: Use one strand of blue.
Starting point: This is indicated on the chart above by an arrow. The first stitch should be made at a point 2 cm (¾ inch) from the right-hand side and 2 cm (¾ inch) from the bottom of the fabric. The long edges are the top and bottom of the fabric, the short edges are the sides.

MAKING UP

Iron the embroidery on the back on a thick towel. The chart has a dotted line to indicate the cutting lines. Count out from the embroidery and carefully cut along the line of holes in the Aida. Fray back by one block, using the tip of a needle to tease out one thread at a time. Decide on the placement of the embroidery on the lid of your chosen box, and stick neatly into position using either stick glue or double-sided tape.

Variations

Work the design on 11 or 14 count fabric for use with larger boxes.

Mount the design, omitting the outer border, in a rectangular keyring fob, 5 x 6.5 cm (2 x 2¾ inches). Follow the making up instructions for the Serpent and Knot keyrings on page 45.

SILVER TRISKELE BOX

The triskele is a three-armed whirligig. It was a sacred Celtic symbol combining two significant elements – the mystic number three and the idea of rotation. For pagan Celts, the rotation of the sun and the seasons was very important. Its tripartite form made it easy to connect the triskele with the Christian concept of the trinity in later Celtic art.

Level **✳✳✳**. The stitched design is 40 x 42 stitches, approximately 6 x 6 cm (2½ x 2½ inches).

YOU WILL NEED:

- ✻ Fabric: 18 count Aida fabric in cream, 15 x 15 cm (6 x 6 inches)
- ✻ Tapestry needle: size: 26
- ✻ Round box: preferably with 65 mm (2½ inch) diameter lid to hold the embroidered top

- ✻ Thread: DMC 6-strand embroidery thread and DMC metallic thread in the following colours and quantities:

Symbol	Colour	Shade	Skeins
●	Dark Blue (2 strands)	820	1
◆	Dark Blue (1 strand)	820	
△	Metallic Silver	5283	1

STITCHING INSTRUCTIONS

Order of working: Mark the top of the fabric with a knot of thread. First stitch the outlines of the circles and whorls in backstitch. Next, fill in the cross stitch areas. Lastly, work the backstitch details on the circles.

Cross stitch: Use one strand of dark blue embroidery thread or one strand of metallic silver for all the cross stitch, except the dark blue stitches at the centre of the circles, which are worked with two strands.

Backstitch: Use two strands of dark blue for all the backstitch, except the centre circle. For this, the three segment outlines are worked using two strands of dark blue, but the left-hand segment is filled in with backstitch using one strand of dark blue, and the lower segment with backstitch using one strand of metallic silver. These infill backstitches are indicated on the chart by dotted lines.

Starting point: This is indicated on the chart below by an arrow. The first stitch is a backstitch and should be made at a point 8 cm (3 inches) from the right-hand side and 4.5 cm (2 inches) from the bottom of the fabric.

MAKING UP

Iron the embroidery on the back on a thick towel. Carefully insert the embroidery into the lid of the box following the manufacturer's instructions. If you are unable to source a suitable box, construct your own box or modify a ready-made one. If using a box with a larger diameter, increase the size of the fabric accordingly.

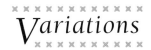

Variations

As this design is ideal for round projects, it could be used with a variety of the items available especially for embroidery, such as handbag mirrors, paperweights and coasters.

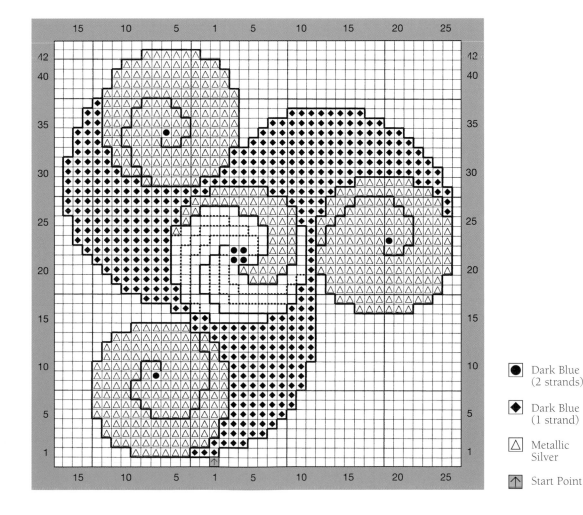

● Dark Blue (2 strands)

◆ Dark Blue (1 strand)

△ Metallic Silver

↑ Start Point

SAINT AND BIRDS ICON

Each of the four evangelists – Matthew, Mark, Luke and John – was often symbolized by an animal or bird. This is John, whose symbol was an eagle. The most magnificent pages in an illuminated manuscript were often the introductory pages to each gospel. The saint sits enthroned on the page, surrounded by richly detailed symbols and borders. John holds a book in his hands – the gospel he has written for the faithful.

Level ✳. The stitched design is 51 x 84 stitches, approximately 9.5 x 15.5 cm (3¾ x 6¼ inches).

YOU WILL NEED:

* Fabric: 14 count Aida fabric in pale grey, size 25 x 30 cm (10 x 12 inches)
* Tapestry needle: size 24
* Frame: suggested aperture size 12.5 x 18 cm (5 x 7 inches)
* Mount and masking tape (optional)
* Thread: DMC 6-strand embroidery thread and DMC metallic thread in the following colours and quantities:

Symbol	Colour	Shade	Skeins
⊞	Very Dark Grey	413	1
✳	Dark Grey	414	1
⊠	Mid Grey	415	1
⊞	Pale Grey	762	1
▲	Dark Gold	832	2
◯	Pale Gold	834	1
●	Cream	746	1
◆	Metallic Gold	5282	1

STITCHING INSTRUCTIONS

Cross stitch: Use three strands of the embroidery thread and one strand of the metallic thread.

Backstitch: Use three strands of dark gold to outline the birds' heads and the saint's halo. Use two strands of very dark grey for all the birds' beaks and eyes, the top eagle's details, the saint's features and the book details.

Starting point: This is indicated on the chart overleaf by an arrow. The first stitch should be made at a point 7.5 cm (3 inches) from the right-hand side and 7.5 cm (3 inches) from the bottom of the fabric.

MAKING UP

Iron the embroidery on the back on a thick towel. Choose a suitable frame. For the frame shown here, the embroidery was stretched around a piece of firm card cut to size, stuck into place with masking tape and mounted in the centre of the frame. Alternatively, mount the embroidery in a traditional gold frame. If using a card mount with your chosen frame, follow the suggestions for making up the Fish and Wave Sampler on page 32.

Variations

Work the other saint and angel designs provided in this chapter as pictures in complementary colours, to make a small group of glowing icons.

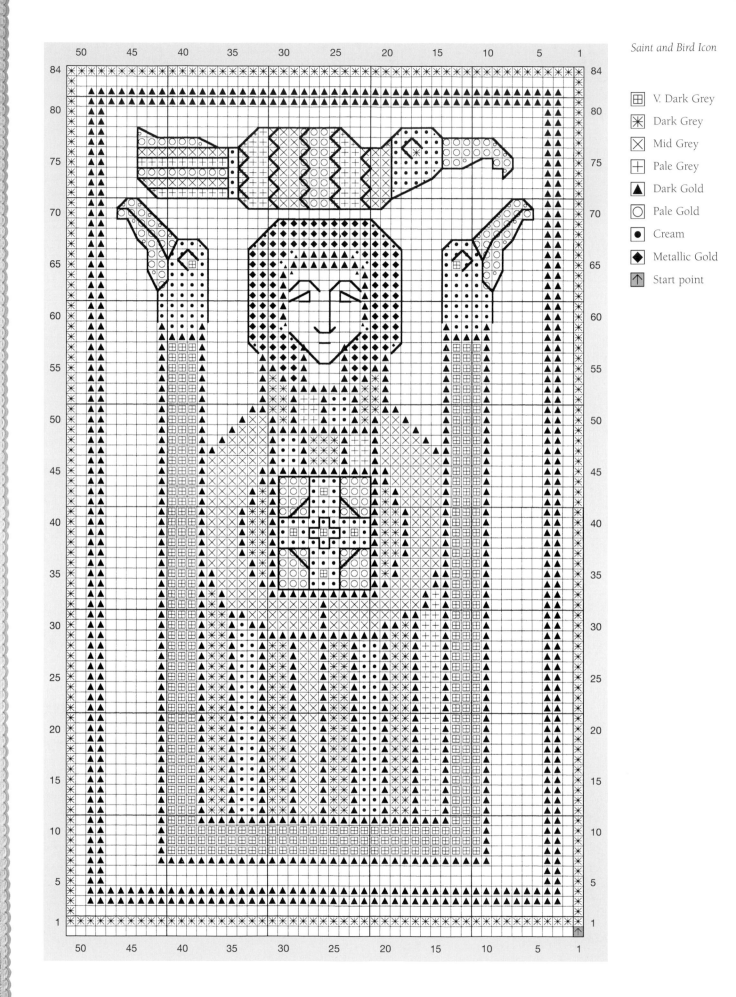

Key:

- ⊞ V. Dark Grey
- ✳ Dark Grey
- ⊠ Mid Grey
- ⊞ Pale Grey
- ▲ Dark Gold
- ○ Pale Gold
- • Cream
- ◆ Metallic Gold
- ↑ Start point

CELTIC SWAN NEEDLECASE

Caer, a beautiful young girl, sang to Aengus in his dreams. He almost died from unrequited love, before he searched and eventually found her with fifty other maidens, all changed into swans. He recognized her by the golden chain around her neck. After many trials, she eventually became his wife, after he had promised that she could change back into a swan whenever she wished.

Level ✳. The stitched design is 45 x 95 stitches, approximately 8 x 17.5 cm (3 x 7 inches).

YOU WILL NEED:

* Fabric: 14 count Aida fabric in cream, 14 x 23 cm (5½ x 9 inches)
* Tapestry needle: size 24 and a sharp sewing needle
* White cardboard
* Felt: 2 pieces in gold, 9 x 18 cm (3½ x 7 inches)
* Tassel or cord: in gold for trimming (optional)

* Thread: DMC 6-strand embroidery thread in the following colours and quantities:

Symbol	Colour	Shade	Skeins
⊞	Dark Gold	832	1
✳	Mid Gold	3820	1
▲	Pale Gold	3821	1
◇	Very Pale Gold	745	1
●	Cream	3823	1
■	Brown	830	1

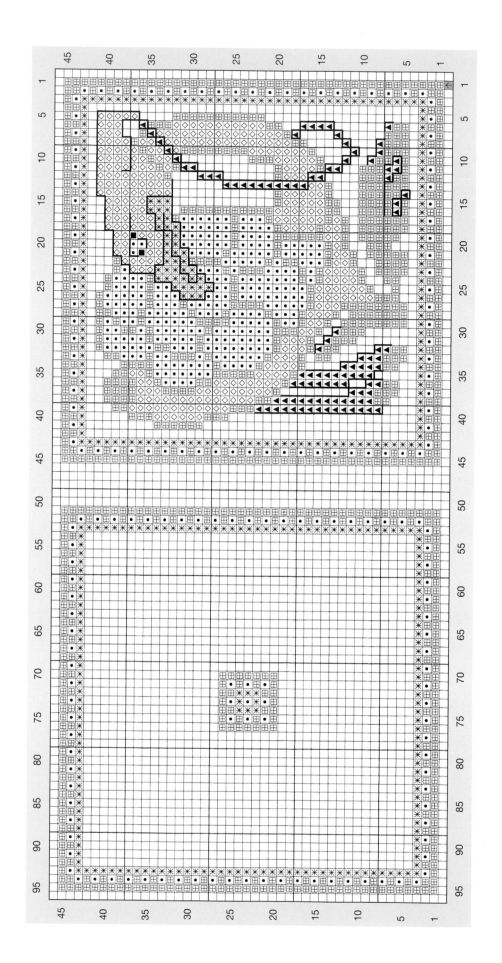

Dark Gold
Mid Gold
Pale Gold
Very Pale Gold
Cream
Brown
Start point

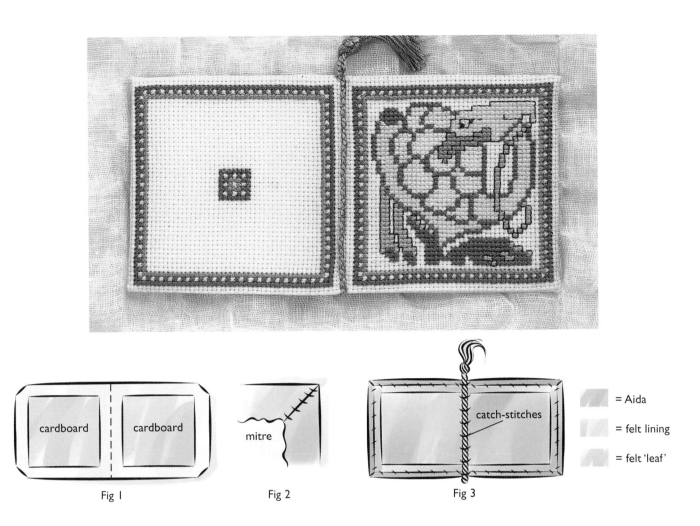

Fig 1   Fig 2   Fig 3

= Aida

= felt lining

= felt 'leaf'

STITCHING INSTRUCTIONS

Cross stitch: Use three strands of the embroidery thread.

Backstitch: Use one strand of brown.

Starting point: This is indicated on the chart by an arrow. The first stitch should be made at a point 2.5 cm (1 inch) from the right-hand side and 2.5 cm (1 inch) from the bottom of the fabric. The long edges are the top and bottom of the needlecase, the short edges are the sides.

MAKING UP

Iron the embroidery on the back on a thick towel. If necessary, iron the felt with a very cool iron. Cut two squares of cardboard slightly larger than one embroidered panel. Place the embroidery face down and position the two pieces of card over the back of the embroidery, leaving a gap of about 1.5 cm (½ inch) between them at the centre (Fig 1). Trim the corners slightly. Fold and iron the edges of the Aida over the

cardboard, two blocks out from the stitched border. Mitre and stitch down the corners using one strand of cream thread (Fig 2). Trim one piece of the felt so it is slightly smaller than the finished needlecase. Sew to the back of the needlecase using a single strand of the nearest colour gold embroidery thread. Trim the second piece of felt so it is slightly smaller than the first – this will be the 'leaf'. Sew into place along the centre spine on the inside of the needlecase. A tassel and cord trimming for the outer and inner spine makes an attractive finishing touch (Fig 3).

✕✕✕✕✕✕✕✕✕✕✕
Variations
✕✕✕✕✕✕✕✕✕✕

Create a matching set of needlework items for your workbox. Using the swan design, stitch a pincushion on 14 count Aida and a scissor keep on 18 count. Follow the making up details for the Celtic Angel Pincushion on page 58 and the Bird-Headed Triskele Scissor Keep on page 79.

CELTIC KNOT BROOCH AND BUTTONS

The knot is the most characteristic motif of Celtic art. It varies from simple shapes, such as those used here, to the elaborate and sinuous interwoven forms of a page in the Book of Kells. *It was common for geometric designs to be significant in cultures that forbade the representation of the human form, such as pagan Celtic society. This love of interlocking shapes was continued into Christian Celtic art.*

Level ✳✳. The stitched design is 19 x 19 stitches and can be worked on a variety of fabrics and in various colourways, using up scraps of fabric and threads. The finished size depends on the fabric used.

YOU WILL NEED:

✳ Fabric: here we used 14 or 18 count Aida and 28 count evenweave fabric, approximately 10 x 10 cm (4 x 4 inches)

✳ Tapestry needle: size 24 or 26

✳ Round brooch: 32 mm (1¼ inch) diameter, suitable for inserting an embroidery, use 18 count Aida worked over one block and size 26 tapestry needle

✳ Large button mould: 38 mm (1½ inch) diameter, use 14 count Aida worked over one block and size 24 tapestry needle, or 28 count evenweave worked over two threads and size 26 tapestry needle

✳ Small button mould: 23 mm (1 inch) diameter, use 28 evenweave worked over one thread and size 26 tapestry needle

✳ Thread: DMC 6-strand embroidery thread and DMC metallic thread in the following colours and quantities (the gold colourway is shown in brackets):

Sym.	Colour	Shade	Skeins
✳	Dark Grey (Dark Gold)	932 (832)	1
△	Pale Grey (Mid Gold)	3753 (3820)	1
●	Metallic Silver (Pale Gold)	5283 (745)	1

STITCHING INSTRUCTIONS

Cross stitch: Depending on the fabric chosen, work as follows:

14 count Aida worked over one block or 28 count evenweave worked over two threads: use two strands of the embroidery thread and one strand of the metallic thread

28 count evenweave worked over one thread: use one strand of the embroidery thread. This count is not suitable for metallic thread.

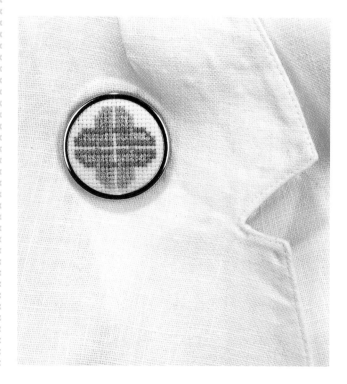

Starting point: Fold the fabric in half and half again to find the centre. Mark the centre of the fabric, and start stitching here from the centre of the knot design.

MAKING UP

Iron the embroideries on the back on a thick towel. Follow the manufacturers' instructions to insert the embroidery into the brooch or to cover the buttons. Use two buttons to embellish the fold of a plain linen cushion, or sew a single button tightly through the centre of a small cushion as shown below.

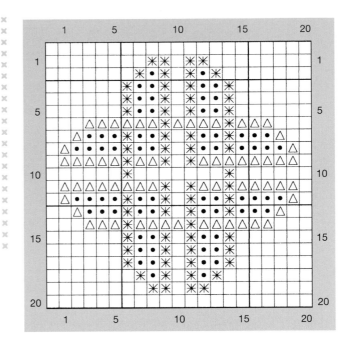

 Dark Grey (Dark Gold)

△ Pale Grey (Mid Gold)

● Metallic Silver (Pale Gold)

DURROW SAINT SACHET

The Book of Durrow is one of the oldest of the surviving Celtic illuminated manuscripts. It dates from the seventh century AD and is named after the monastery founded by St Columba in Co. Offaly, Ireland. At the beginning of the book, a page illustrates each of the four evangelists. This design is inspired by one of them. The evangelist has a wonderful naive, geometric simplicity. The style shows an art form not yet totally comfortable with the depiction of the human figure.

Level ✱✱. The stitched size is 26 x 79 stitches, approximately 4.5 x 13.25 cm (1¾ x 5¼ inches).

YOU WILL NEED:

* Fabric: 35 cm (14 inches) of 5 cm (2 inch) wide Aida band in gold
* Tapestry needle: size 24 and a sharp sewing needle
* Sewing thread: in gold to match the Aida band
* Fabric: to make inner sachet bag for pot pourri
* Pot pourri
* Narrow ribbon: 50 cm (20 inches) long
* Thread: DMC 6-strand embroidery thread and DMC metallic thread in the following colours and quantities:

Symbol	Colour	Shade	Skeins
✳	Tan	918	1
☐	Brown	3021	1
◆	Green	924	1
△	Metallic Copper	5279	1

STITCHING INSTRUCTIONS

Cross stitch: Use three strands of the embroidery thread and one strand of the metallic thread.

Backstitch: The metallic backstitch is indicated on the chart by dotted lines, and the remaining brown and tan backstitch by solid black lines. Work the backstitch in the following order when the cross stitch is complete. Use two strands of tan to outline the tan check blocks, the centre strip, the shoulders and the hem of the saint's robe. Use one strand of metallic copper to work the squares within the grid blocks, and to work the diagonals over the two brown blocks. Use two strands of brown to work the diagonals on the two bottom grid blocks, the outlines of the feet, hair and face. Use one strand of brown for the diagonals on the remaining grid blocks and for the facial features.

Starting point: This is indicated on the chart by an arrow. Fold the Aida band in half. The first stitch should be made at a point 3 cm (1¼ inches) up from centre fold of the fabric and over the first block from the right. First work the tan blocks across the width of the fabric, using the full 26 blocks of the Aida band.

MAKING UP

Iron the embroidery on the back on a thick towel. Iron folds in the band two blocks above and below the stitched area. Fold in the top of the sachet at the back to the same size as the front. Fold the inside turnings away from the sides. From the right side, using gold sewing thread, stitch the sides together with small running stitches just inside the scalloped borders.

Make an inner sachet bag slightly smaller than the size of the finished sachet. This is filled with the pot pourri, and prevents the oils damaging the embroidery. Thread the ribbon through the centre of the embroidered circle at the top of the sachet and through the back of the sachet. Knot and tie into a decorative bow and loop over the matching hanger (see page 77).

Variations

Work this design as a bookmark by lengthening the vertical rows of stitches in the arch shape above the saint's head. Finish in the same way as the Eagle Bookmark on page 60.

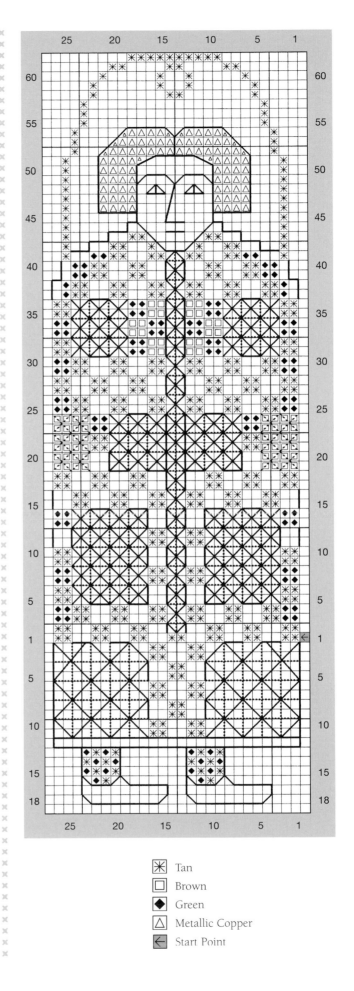

⊞ Tan
☐ Brown
◆ Green
△ Metallic Copper
← Start Point

DURROW KNOT CLOTHES HANGER

A Celtic knot was an image of eternity, infinitely scrolling upon itself. Although, like the matching sachet, these knots are inspired by the page of the Book of Durrow *illustrated on page 56, they have been adapted to a more manageable, and finite, double knot.*

Level **✷✷**. The stitched size of each knot repeat is 22 x 56 stitches, about 3.5 x 9.5 cm (1½ x 3¾ inches).

YOU WILL NEED:

✷ Padded clothes hanger
✷ Fabric: 5 cm (2 inch) wide Aida band in gold, the length of your hanger plus 10 cm (4 inches)
✷ Tapestry needle: size 24 and a sharp sewing needle
✷ Felt: sufficient to cover the hanger completely
✷ Sewing thread: to match felt and gold Aida band
✷ Thread: DMC 6-strand embroidery thread and DMC metallic thread in the following colours and quantities:

Symbol	Colour	Shade	Skeins
◇	Tan	918	1
▲	Brown	3021	1
✳	Green	924	1
	Metallic Copper	5279	1

STITCHING INSTRUCTIONS

Preparation: We used a small clothes hanger, and worked just two knots on the Aida band, with a space between them where the sachet will hang. Using the measurements above for each knot, work out how many knots will fit your hanger. Do not place the knots too close to the ends of the hanger. Note that the two knots on the charts overleaf have been flipped over to provide a symmetrical design. If you cannot balance your knots in this way, just repeat the one knot with suitable spacings.

Cross stitch: Use three strands of the embroidery thread and one strand of the metallic thread.

Backstitch: On the charts overleaf, the metallic back-stitch is indicated by a dotted line, and the brown backstitch by a solid black line. First, use one strand to work the metallic copper, and then work the grid over it with one strand of brown.

Starting point: This is indicated on the charts by an arrow. The first stitch should be made over the third block from one edge of the Aida band and a suitable distance from one end of the band.

MAKING UP

Iron the embroidery on the back on a thick towel. If necessary, iron the felt with a very cool iron. Cut the felt to a rectangle approximately 5 cm (2 inches) longer and wider than the length and girth of the hanger. Sew the felt tightly over the hanger to cover it completely. The seams should be to the centre front. Tack Aida band to the felt on the front of the hanger. Tuck in the ends of the band neatly. Stitch into place with small invisible stitches.

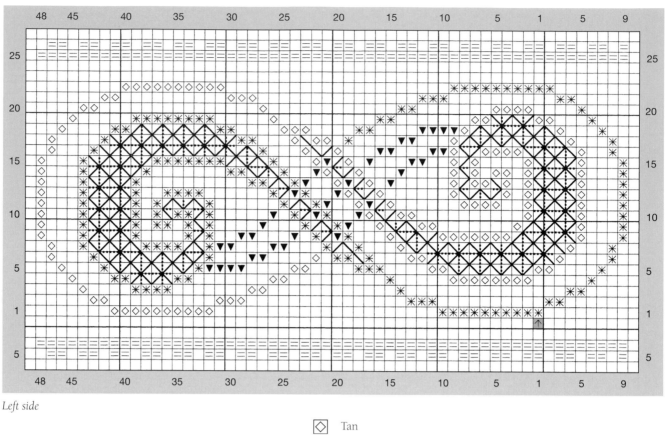

Left side

Durrow Knot Clothes Hanger

◇ Tan
▼ Brown
✳ Green
= Aida Band Edge
↑ Start Point

Right side

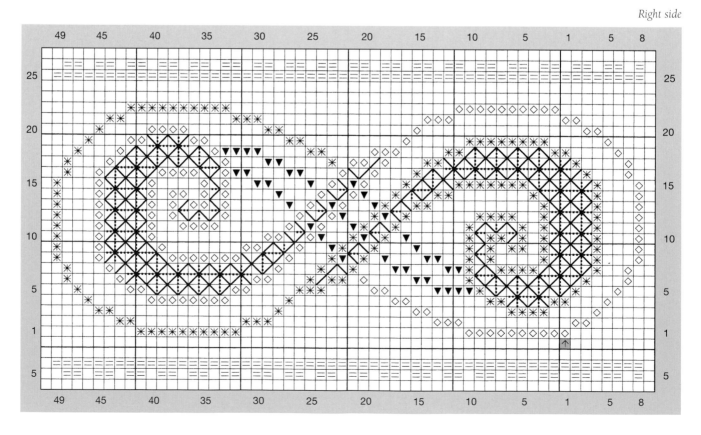

BIRD-HEADED TRISKELE SCISSOR KEEP

The Celts loved the idea of shifting shapes. In many legends the hero is changed into an animal or bird, and back again. They also liked to hide animal forms within geometric shapes. In this design, the magical whirling arms of the triskele end in three bird heads. A triskele was a protection from evil spirits.

Level ✳. The stitched design is 51 x 55 stitches, approximately 7 x 8 cm (2¾ x 3¼ inches).

YOU WILL NEED:

✳ Fabric: 18 count Aida fabric in cream: 2 pieces each 15 x 15 cm (6 x 6 inches)

✳ Tapestry needle: size 26 and a sharp sewing needle

✳ Cord: in gold, a length of 38 cm (15 inches). Alternatively, make a cord by plaiting lengths of embroidery thread

✳ Stuffing

✳ Thread: DMC 6-strand embroidery thread in the following colours and quantities:

Symbol	Colour	Shade	Skeins
⊠	Dark Gold	832	1
◆	Mid Gold	3820	1
▼	Pale Gold	745	1
⊙	Cream	3823	1
	Brown	830	1

STITCHING INSTRUCTIONS

Cross stitch: Use two strands of embroidery thread .
Backstitch: Use one strand of brown.
Starting point: This is indicated on the chart on page 81 by an arrow. The first stitch should be made at a point 4 cm (1½ inches) from the right-hand side and 4 cm (1½ inches) from the bottom of the fabric.

MAKING UP

Iron the embroidery on the back on a thick towel. Place the second piece of Aida over the front. Pin the right sides together. Using a single strand of cream and small backstitches, stitch the two pieces together, two blocks (or the equivalent) out from the outer triangle. Leave two gaps, one of 5 cm (2 inches) in the base of the triangle, and the other at the top of the triangle for inserting the cord. Trim away the excess Aida fabric and turn the scissor keep to the right side through the large gap. Gently pull out the tips of the triangle using a blunt needle. Stuff, then sew up the gap. Insert the two ends of the cord through the top gap, as shown in the photo overleaf, and secure.

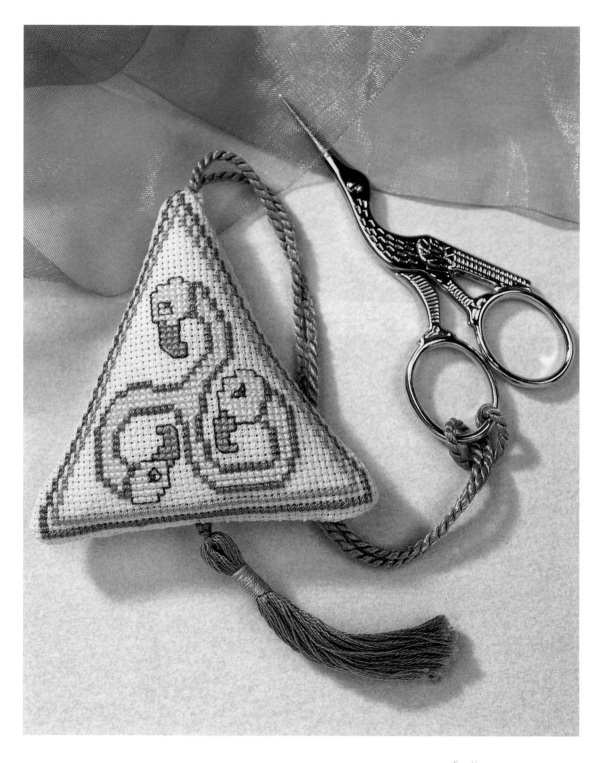

To make the tassel, cut twelve 13 cm (5 inch) lengths of dark gold. Tie them together firmly in the middle with a further 30 cm (12 inch) length of dark gold. Fold over and wrap tightly together with a 30 cm (12 inch) length of mid gold. Sew the end of the wrap into the tassel and trim. Sew the tassel to the centre of the triangle base. Loop the cord through a pair of scissors.

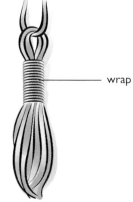

wrap

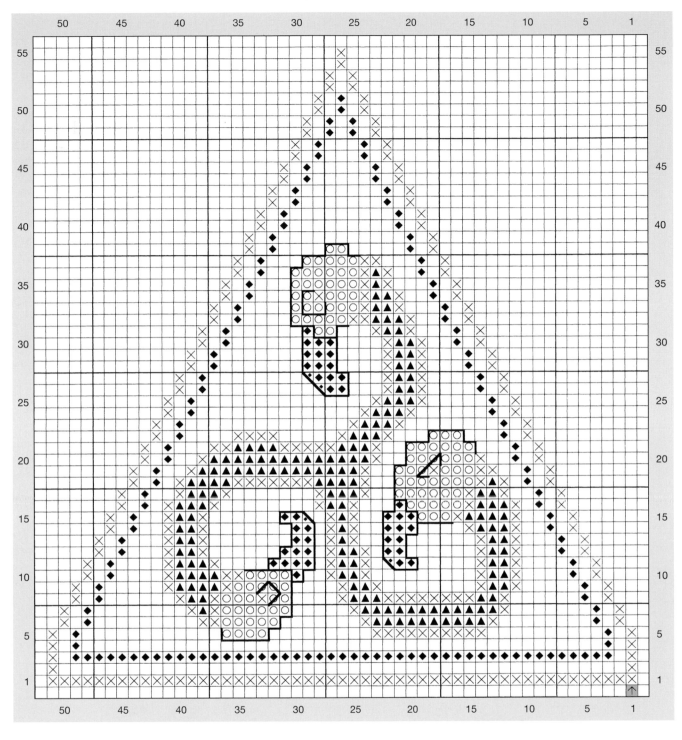

	Dark Gold
◆	Mid Gold
▲	Pale Gold
○	Cream
↑	Start Point

Variations

For a very different look, work the bird-headed triskele in the rich colours of a Celtic manuscript, such as the rich bronzes used for the Durrow Saint Sachet featured on page 74.

Celtic art inspired by the natural world.

CARTH

Earth was the life-giving soil - to grow crops to feed man and beast. It was governed by the all-important seasons, by the cycle of planting and harvest, of birth and death. Rock was hewn from the earth and raised as standing stones, again to mark the passing of time with ritual and sacrifice. Rocks were carved with spirals and knots to express the continuity and infinite complexity of the life-giving forces.

THE DESIGNS

Many of the projects in this section are inspired by the carved details found on Celtic crosses. Our choice of motifs emphasizes the diversity of inspiration of Celtic art. Designs were adapted from many sources, and survived long after the original source of the inspiration had disappeared. For example, the vine comes from an early period when the Celts were living in Mediterranean areas, in contact with Greeks and Romans. The Lewis chessmen show the mingling of Celtic and Viking art at a very late date. This chapter also demonstrates the adaptability of cross stitch motifs. A trailing vine can be sewn along a tablemat, or a small detail used to embellish the corner of a napkin.

VINE CARD

The long continuity of Celtic art is apparent in the use of vine motifs in the illuminated manuscripts of Scotland and Ireland, far from any growing vine. It shows the far-reaching influence of early Mediterranean, classical and even Egyptian art on the Celts. The lotus and palmette endured as images in a similar way.

Level **✱**. The stitched design is 30 x 30 stitches, approximately 5.5 x 5.5 cm (2¼ x 2¼ inches).

YOU WILL NEED:

* Fabric: 14 count Aida fabric in cream, 13 x 13 cm (5 x 5 inches)
* Tapestry needle: size 24
* Card in purple, cut to size 11 x 22 cm (4¼ x 8½ inches)
* Steel rule and craft knife
* Stick glue or double-sided tape
* Thread: DMC 6-strand embroidery thread in the following colours and quantities:

Symbol	Colour	Shade	Skeins
▲	Dark Purple	550	1
◯	Pale Purple	333	1
☒	Green	470	1
⦿	Grey	415	1

STITCHING INSTRUCTIONS

Cross stitch: Use three strands of embroidery thread.
Starting point: This is indicated on the chart by an arrow. The first stitch should be made at a point 3.5 cm (1½ inches) from the right-hand side and 3.5 cm (1½ inches) from the bottom of the fabric.

MAKING UP

Iron the embroidery on the back on a thick towel. The chart has a dotted line to indicate the cutting lines. Count out from the embroidery and carefully cut along the lines of the holes in the Aida. Fray back by two blocks, using the tip of a needle to tease out one

thread at a time. Using a steel rule and a craft knife, lightly score and then fold the card to give a folded size of 11 x 11 cm (4¼ x 4¼ inches). Stick the embroidery centrally on the card using stick glue or double-sided tape.

POT POURRI SACHET

Stitch this design onto wide Aida band to make a small pot pourri sachet or pincushion.

YOU WILL NEED:

* Fabric: 20 cm (8 inch) length of 8 cm (3 inch) wide Aida band in cream
* Sewing thread: in cream

* Lining fabric: in cream, 9 x 18 cm (3½ x 7 inches) to make an inner lining, if filling with pot pourri
* Stuffing (if making a pincushion)
* Thread: as for the card

STITCHING INSTRUCTIONS

Cross stitch: Use three strands of embroidery thread.
Starting point: This is indicated on the chart by an arrow. The first stitch should be made over the seventh block from the right-hand side and 4 cm (1½ inches) from the bottom of the band.

MAKING UP

Iron the embroidery on the back on a thick towel. Fold right sides together 1.5 cm (½ inch) from the embroidered border. Using cream sewing thread, sew the two layers together at the same distance from the opposite border. Trim the ragged ends. Turn right side out. Turn in the corners neatly and stitch along one edge using small running stitches. Fill with stuffing or

pot pourri (make a small bag from the cream lining fabric to hold the pot pourri as the oils may stain your embroidery). Sew up the remaining side, turning in the corners neatly.

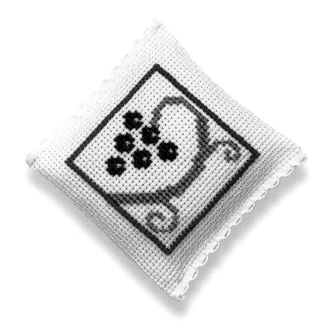

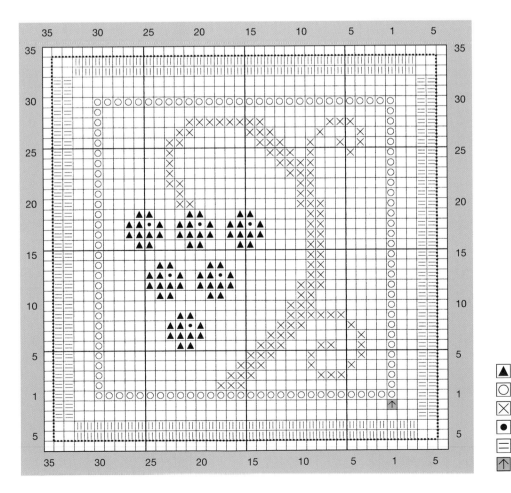

	Dark Purple
○	Pale Purple
✕	Green
•	Grey
⊟	Frayed Edge
↑	Start Point

VINE PLACEMAT

Patterns of meandering tendrils based on vine-stems, often transformed into pure design, adorn metalwork and stones found throughout the Celtic world. Bunches of grapes, symbolizing communion wine, appear in illuminated manuscripts.

Level **✱✱**. The stitched size of each repeat is 26 x 53 stitches, approximately 4.5 x 9 cm (1¾ x 3½ inches).

YOU WILL NEED:

* ✱ Placemat
* ✱ Fabric: 5 cm (2 inch) wide Aida band in cream. Find the length needed by measuring the depth of your placemat and adding 12 cm (5 inches).
* ✱ Tapestry needle: size 24 and a sharp sewing needle
* ✱ Sewing thread: in cream to match the Aida band
* ✱ Thread: DMC 6-strand embroidery thread in the following colours and quantities:

Symbol	Colour	Shade	Skeins
▲	Dark Purple	550	1
◯	Pale Purple	333	1
⊠	Green	470	1
⊙	Grey	415	1

STITCHING INSTRUCTIONS

Cross stitch: Use three strands of embroidery thread.

Starting point: This is indicated on the chart by an arrow. Fold the Aida band in half to find the centre. The first stitch should be made on this fold and over the first block from the right-hand side. Work the green stems upwards and finish at an appropriate point in the design, approximately 7 cm (2¾ inches) from the top of the band. Work down from the start point in the same way. Finally, work the bunches of grapes, leaving out any incomplete bunches.

MAKING UP

Iron the embroidery on the back on a thick towel. Trim the ends of the Aida band so that it is 5 cm (2 inches) longer than the depth of the placemat. Fold over a 1.5 cm (½ inch) turning to the wrong side of the Aida band and iron. Position the band on the

placemat, turning the ends to the back, and pin in place. Stitch down each side of the band, taking care not to sew over the embroidery. Hand stitch the ends at the back.

Variations

This band could be used to decorate a cushion. Use traditional Celtic colours of glowing ochres, rusty red and verdigris, stitched on a vellum-coloured band.

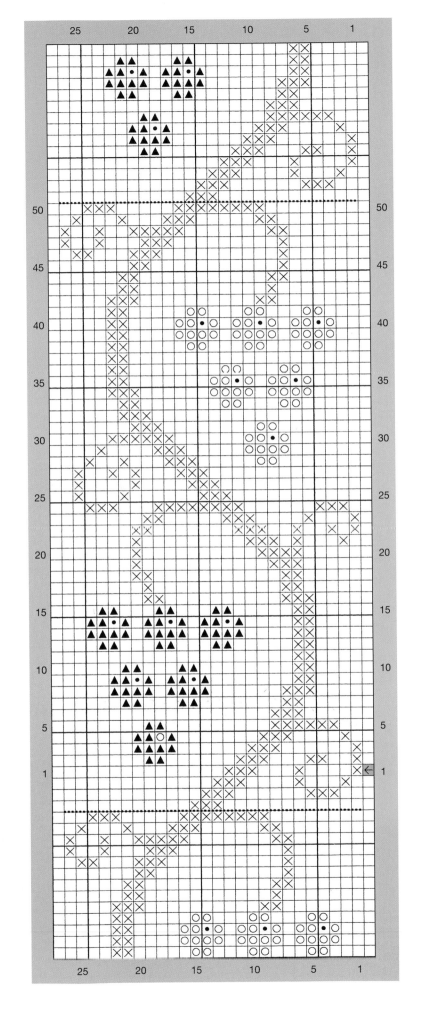

▲	Dark Purple
O	Pale Purple
☒	Green
●	Grey
←	Start Point

VINE NAPKIN

Early Celtic society in Europe set great store on feasting and festivals, and elaborately decorated drinking vessels have been found in many early graves. Drinking horns and a beautiful gold bowl and ladle were discovered in the tomb of one chieftain. Appropriately, drinking vessels were often decorated with vines.

Level **✳✳✳**. The stitched design is 32 x 45 stitches, approximately 5.5 x 7 cm (2¼ x 2¾ inches).

YOU WILL NEED:

* Napkin: in cream
* Waste canvas: 14 count, 11 x 13 cm (4¼ x 5 inches)
* Tacking thread
* Sharp needle
* Thread: DMC 6-strand embroidery thread in the following colours and quantities:

Symbol	Colour	Shade	Skeins
▲	Dark Purple	550	1
✕	Green	470	1
●	Grey	415	1

STITCHING INSTRUCTIONS

Waste canvas: Position the waste canvas diagonally in one corner of the napkin, as shown by the dotted lines on the chart, and carefully tack it down.

Cross stitch: Use three strands of embroidery thread, and work over pairs of threads in the waste canvas.

Starting point: This is indicated on the chart overleaf by an arrow. The first stitch should be made at a point approximately 5 cm (2 inches) from the right-hand side and 3 cm (1¼ inches) from the bottom of the waste canvas. These measurements are approximate as they depend on the size of the hem on your napkin.

MAKING UP

When you have finished all the stitching, lay a damp towel over the waste canvas to dissolve the glue holding the threads together. Carefully pull out each thread, leaving only the embroidery on the napkin. Iron the embroidery on the back on a thick towel.

Variations

Waste canvas is useful for stitching onto clothing or any bought item in a close woven fabric. Remember that the canvas has to be dampened to loosen the threads, so only washable fabrics are suitable. Don't be too ambitious in the design you choose. It works best with small simple designs using a limited number of colours. Try stitching a leaf or flower onto a gardening apron, or initials and a heart on a child's blanket.

Vine Napkin

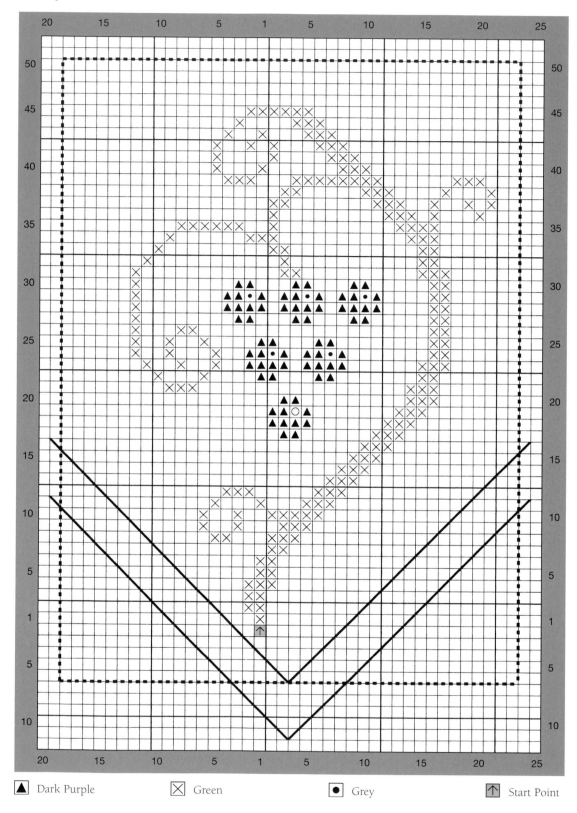

▲ Dark Purple   ☒ Green   ● Grey   ↑ Start Point

SPIRALS CUSHION

Throughout the Celtic lands, sacred places were marked by carved pillars – an expression of energy in imitation of the tree, a potent life symbol for Celts. The patterns on these pillars mimicked the richly decorated 'carpet pages' of illuminated manuscripts, which in turn showed the influence of intricate interlacings from ancient pagan metalwork.

Level ✱. The stitched design is 108 x 108 stitches, approximately 20 x 20 cm (8 x 8 inches).

YOU WILL NEED:

* Fabric: 14 count Aida fabric in taupe, 28 x 28 cm (11 x 11 inches)
* Tapestry needle: size 24 and a sharp sewing needle
* Border fabric: linen fabric in taupe, two pieces 10 x 26 cm (4 x 10¼ inches), and two pieces 10 x 42 cm (4 x 16½ inches)
* Backing fabric: linen fabric in taupe, two pieces 30 x 42 cm (12 x 16½ inches)
* Sewing thread: in taupe, to match linen
* Four large buttons (optional)
* Cushion pad: 35 x 35 cm (14 x 14 inches)
* Thread: DMC 6-strand embroidery thread in the following colours and quantities:

Symbol	Colour	Shade	Skeins
■	Dark Green	730	1
▲	Mid Green	470	1
◇	Pale Green	3819	2
✕	Cream	746	2
⊞	Turquoise	598	1

STITCHING INSTRUCTIONS

Cross stitch: Use three strands of embroidery thread.
Starting point: This is indicated on the chart overleaf by an arrow. The first stitch should be made at a point 4 cm (1½ inches) from the right-hand side and 4 cm (1½ inches) from the bottom of the fabric.

MAKING UP

Iron the embroidery on the back on a thick towel. All the seam allowances are 1 cm (½ inch). Measure out 3 cm (1¼ inches) from the edges of the embroidered border and cut the Aida to this size, cutting along the line of the holes in the fabric. With right sides together, sew the two short border pieces to opposite edges of the Aida (Fig 1, overleaf). Iron the seams open.

With right sides together, sew the two long border pieces on to the other two sides (Fig 2, overleaf). Iron the seams open.

Hem one long side of each of the back pieces. With right sides together, lay the two back pieces over the embroidered front, with the hemmed edges overlapping at the centre. Pin in place and sew all round. Turn right sides out. Sew a decorative button onto each corner, through the front layer only (optional). Iron on the back then insert cushion pad.

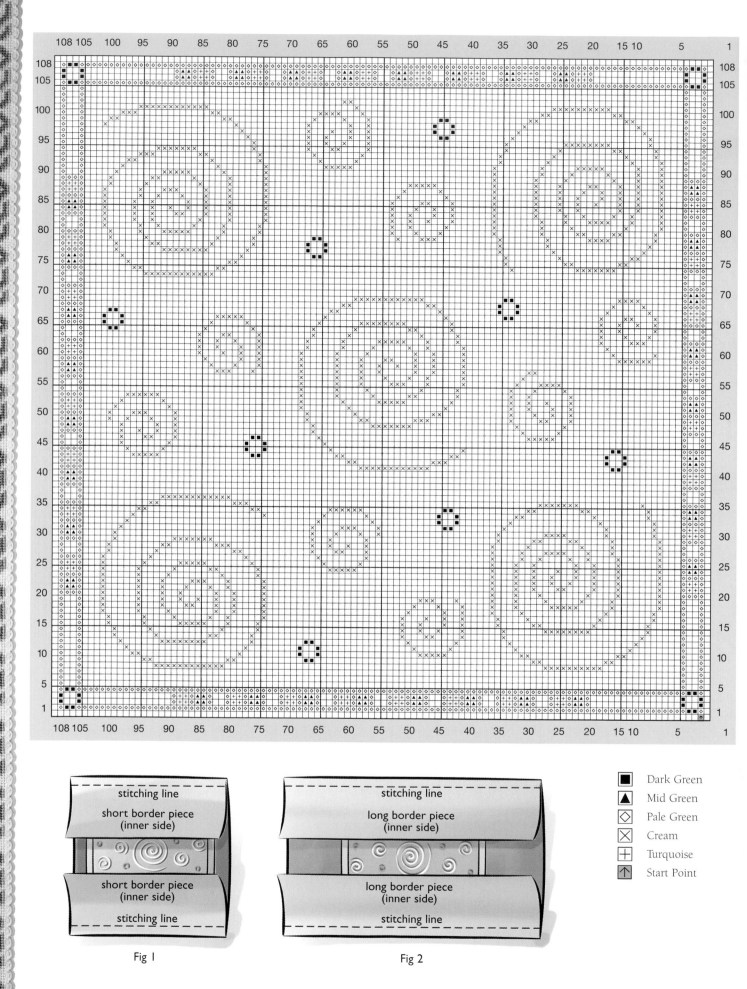

Fig 1

Fig 2

■	Dark Green
▲	Mid Green
◇	Pale Green
✕	Cream
+	Turquoise
↑	Start Point

Fig 1

stitching line

short border piece
(inner side)

short border piece
(inner side)

stitching line

Fig 2

stitching line

long border piece
(inner side)

long border piece
(inner side)

stitching line

SPIRAL CARD

Almost every construction in the natural world is based on spirals and circles, and throughout history these patterns have appeared on decorative art. Early man would have been influenced by the beauty of spirals in shells – the earliest dwellings were round, and key patterns (spirals drawn using straight lines) have been found engraved on mammoth ivory. Egyptians used spirals as decoration, and double spirals appear on bronze age metalwork of the Baltic countries. However, it was the Celts who developed the most complicated double and triple interlocking spirals, covering bronze ornaments, stones and wonderful illuminated manuscripts with fanciful whorls.

Level ✱. The stitched design is 30 x 30 stitches, approximately 5.5 x 5.5 cm (2¼ x 2¼ inches).

YOU WILL NEED:

* Fabric: 14 count Aida fabric in taupe, 13 x 13 cm (5 x 5 inches)
* Tapestry needle: size 24
* Cardboard: in cream, cut to 11 x 22 cm (4¼ x 8½ inches)
* Steel rule and craft knife
* Stick glue or double-sided tape
* Thread: DMC 6-strand embroidery thread in the following colours and quantities (colours used for the large scale Binca version below right are shown in brackets):

Sym.	Colour	Shade	Skeins
⊞	Dark Green (Dark Green)	730 (730)	1
◇	Pale Green (Turquoise)	3819 (598)	1
⊠	Cream (Pale Green)	746 (3819)	1
⊞	Turquoise (Beige)	598 (642)	1

STITCHING INSTRUCTIONS

Cross stitch: Use three strands of embroidery thread.
Starting point: This is indicated on the chart by an arrow. The first stitch should be made at a point 3.5 cm (1½ inches) from the right-hand side and 3.5 cm (1½ inches) from the bottom of the fabric.

MAKING UP

Iron the embroidery on the back on a thick towel. The cutting line is 4 blocks out from the edge of the embroidery. Count out from the embroidery and carefully cut along the lines of the holes in the Aida. Fray back by two blocks, gently using the tip of a needle to tease out one thread at a time. Using a steel rule

⬆ Start Point

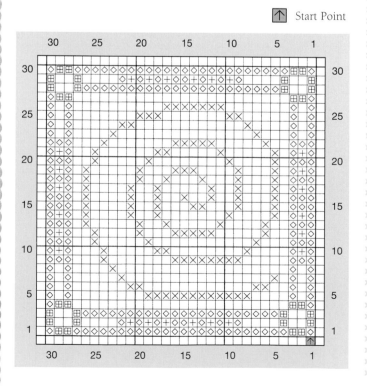

and a craft knife, lightly score and then fold the card to give a folded size of 11 x 11 cm (4¼ x 4¼ inches). Stick the embroidery centrally on the card using stick glue or double-sided tape.

Variations

Stitched on different fabric, this design could be used as a cushion centre, a small mat, a large card, or a picture. Here we have used a very large scale fabric, 6 count Binca in cream, size 20 x 20 cm (8 x 8 inches), to make a picture. For this fabric, use 6 strands of thread and a size 22 needle. The stitched size is 12.5 x 12.5 cm (5 x 5 inches).

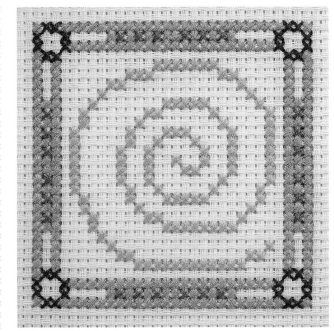

CHESSBOARD

An early Celtic version of the game of chess translates as 'wooden wisdom', and already includes the central idea of the king piece battling across the board. In the twelfth century chess was a game played by the upper classes, both men and women. Chessboards were rare and valuable, sometimes inlaid with gold and silver, and hung on the wall as ornament when not in use.

Level ✱. The stitched design is 175 x 175 stitches, approximately 32 x 32 cm (12½ x 12½ inches). The green stitches are worked over ONE block, and the stone stitches are worked over TWO blocks.

YOU WILL NEED:

* Fabric: 14 count Aida fabric in cream, 48 x 48 cm (19 x 19 inches)
* Tapestry needle: size 24 and a sharp sewing needle
* Sewing thread: in cream to match Aida and to match felt
* Felt: in cream, 35 x 35 cm (14 x 14 inches)
* Thread: DMC 6-strand embroidery thread in the following colours and quantities:

Symbol	Colour	Shade	Skeins
●	Green	907	4
⊠	Stone	642	5

STITCHING INSTRUCTIONS

Cross stitch: Use 3 strands of embroidery thread . Work the green stitches over ONE block and the stone stitches over TWO blocks.

Backstitch: Use two strands of green.

Starting point: This is indicated on the chart by an arrow. The first stitch should be made at a point 8 cm (3 inches) from the right-hand side and 8 cm (3 inches) from the bottom of the fabric. The chart shows the bottom right-hand corner of the board. Repeat the design as shown in the diagram.

MAKING UP

Iron the embroidery on the back on a thick towel. Trim the edges so that they are 5 cm (2 inches) out from the embroidered border, cutting along a line of the holes in the Aida. Fold to the back by 2.5 cm (1 inch). Mitre the corners and stitch neatly to hold in place. Sew the felt to the back of the chessboard.

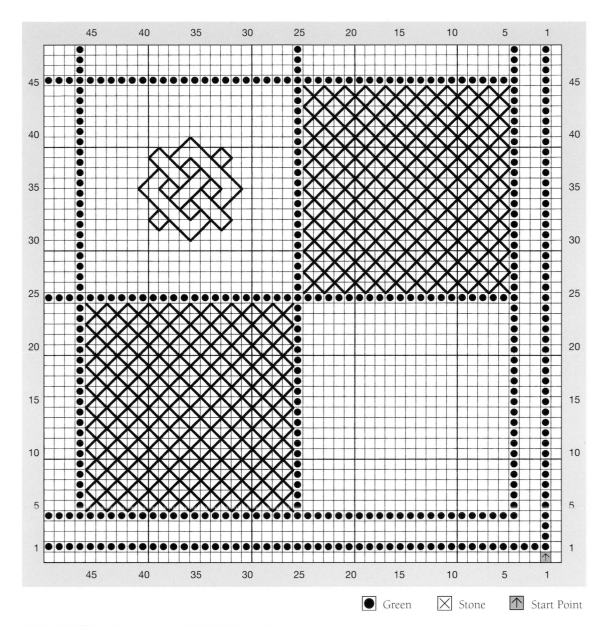

● Green   ☒ Stone   ↑ Start Point

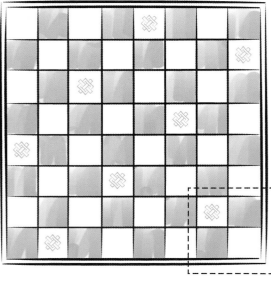

The dotted line shows the area of the chart

Variations

Stitch onto dark Aida using a bright jewel-like colour for the grid and light coloured thread to fill in the squares. Place one backstitched pattern in each of the blank squares. To imitate twelfth-century chessboards, work these using one strand of metallic thread.

LEWIS CHESSMEN BAG

The beautifully carved walrus ivory figures found on the Scottish island of Lewis by 'a peasant of the place, whilst digging a sandbank', as a newspaper reported in 1831, are the finest group of twelfth-century chessmen to have survived. Chess was believed to have been invented by Lugh, the god of fire. Games of chess appear in legends as part of the fight for victory between warring forces.

Level ✱✱✱. The stitched design is 56 x 56 stitches, approximately 11 x 11 cm (4¼ x 4¼ inches). Each stitch in this design is worked over TWO threads.

YOU WILL NEED:

* ✱ Fabric: 28 count evenweave fabric in cream, 26 x 51 cm (10¼ x 20 inches)
* ✱ Tapestry needle: size 26 and a sharp sewing needle
* ✱ Sewing thread: in cream, to match the evenweave
* ✱ Lining fabric: a piece of lightweight fabric in cream, 22 x 47 cm (8¾ x 18½ inches)
* ✱ Embroidery thread: in cream, to match the evenweave
* ✱ 4 small buttons (optional)
* ✱ 2 small pieces of Velcro
* ✱ Thread: DMC 6-strand embroidery thread in the following colours and quantities:

Symbol	Colour	Shade	Skeins
●	Green	907	1
✱	Dark Stone	646	1
◇	Mid Stone	642	1
⊡	Pale Stone	648	1
	Dark Grey	3799	1

STITCHING INSTRUCTIONS

Preparation: Oversew or bind the edges of the evenweave with masking tape before starting to sew to prevent fraying.

Cross stitch: Use two strands of embroidery thread and work each stitch over TWO threads.

Backstitch: Use two strands of dark grey. The backstitch is worked over TWO threads, except the noses which are worked as single long stitches. The downturned corners of the queen's mouth and the highlights in all of the eyes are worked over ONE thread.

Starting point: This is indicated on the chart overleaf by an arrow. The first stitch should be made at a point 7.5 cm (3 inches) from the right-hand long side and 7.5 cm (3 inches) from the top of the fabric.

MAKING UP

Iron the embroidery on the back on a thick towel. Using a ruler and a soft pencil lightly mark cutting lines (see diagram overleaf). Measure from the outer edges of the embroidered square to determine the cutting lines. Measure 5.5 cm (2¼ inches) out from the top (B), right-hand (C) and left-hand (A) edges of the embroidered area, and 30.5 cm (12 inches) from the bottom edge. Cut along these lines. Turn all the edges of the evenweave to the back by 1.5 cm (½ inch), fold in the corners neatly, and iron into place.

Do the same with the lining fabric, but turn over a little more on each edge so that it is slightly smaller than the evenweave. With wrong sides together, place the lining on top of the evenweave, pin, and stitch round all the edges neatly by hand.

Fold at the points marked on the diagram and iron into place. Open out again and sew on a small decorative button in the positions shown on the diagram overleaf (optional). Fold up again, pin the side seams and oversew. Add Velcro to fasten the flap.

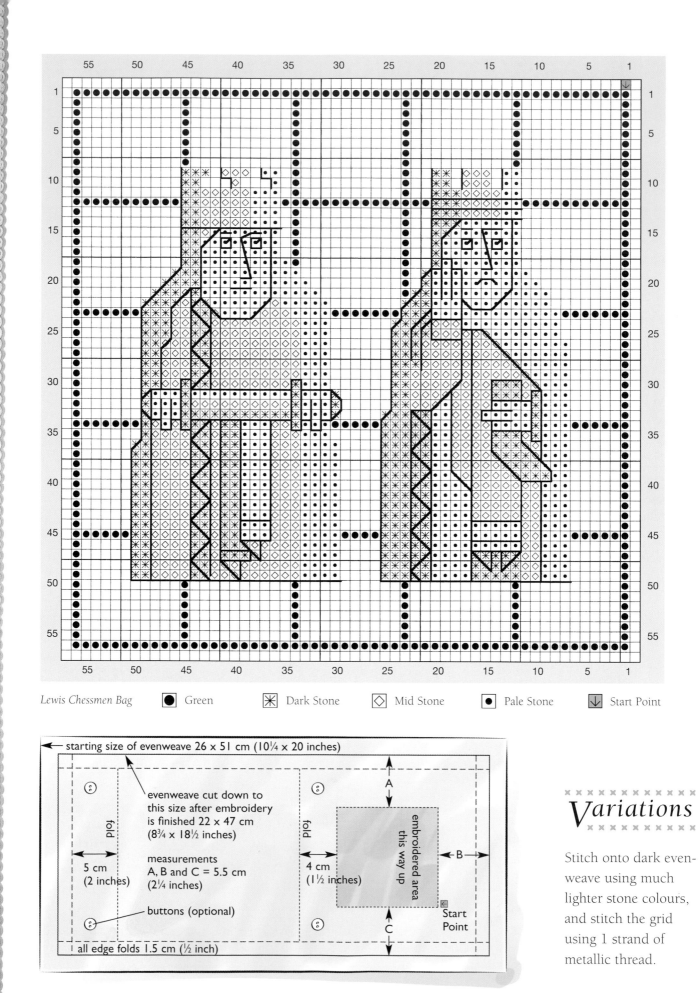

Lewis Chessmen Bag   ● Green   ✳ Dark Stone   ◇ Mid Stone   • Pale Stone   ↓ Start Point

← starting size of evenweave 26 x 51 cm (10¼ x 20 inches)

evenweave cut down to
this size after embroidery
is finished 22 x 47 cm
(8¾ x 18½ inches)

fold

5 cm
(2 inches)

measurements
A, B and C = 5.5 cm
(2¼ inches)

buttons (optional)

fold

4 cm
(1½ inches)

A

embroidered area
this way up

B

C

Start
Point

all edge folds 1.5 cm (½ inch)

Variations

Stitch onto dark even-
weave using much
lighter stone colours,
and stitch the grid
using 1 strand of
metallic thread.

CHESS CARD

This pattern is carved on a pawn (or footsoldier), one of the ancient chess pieces found on the wild Atlantic coastline of the Isle of Lewis. From the eighth century, Viking raids threatened the established Celtic culture of Scotland and Ireland. However, the two traditions enriched each other artistically, and Celtic treasures have been found in many Scandinavian graves.

Level ✱. The stitched design is 30 x 30 stitches, approximately 5.5 x 5.5 cm (2¼ x 2¼ inches).

YOU WILL NEED:

* Fabric: 14 count Aida fabric in taupe, 13 x 13 cm (5 x 5 inches)
* Tapestry needle: size 24
* Card: in cream, cut to size 11 x 22 cm (4¼ x 8½ inches)
* Stick glue or double-sided tape
* Thread: DMC 6-strand embroidery thread in the following colours and quantities:

Symbol	Colour	Shade	Skeins
●	Green	907	1
	Cream	746	1

STITCHING INSTRUCTIONS

Cross Stitch: Use three strands of embroidery thread.
Backstitch: Use three strands of cream.
Starting point: This is indicated on the chart by an arrow. The first stitch should be made at a point 3.5 cm (1½ inches) from the right-hand side and 3.5 cm (1½ inches) from the bottom of the fabric.

MAKING UP

Follow the Making Up instructions for the Spiral Card on page 94

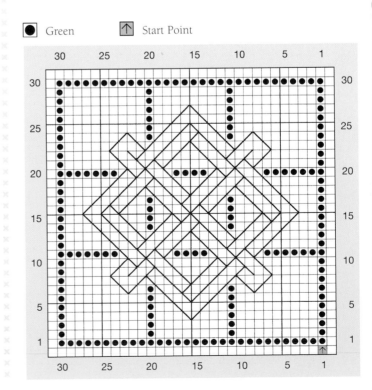

● Green   ↑ Start Point

CELTIC CROSS PICTURE

Celtic design combined with Christian motifs to produce a style rich with intricate patterns and symbolism. By the seventh century, rough standing stones had evolved into finely wrought crosses and were the main ornament of monasteries, although they were still sculpted with traditional pagan Celtic motifs of spirals and triskeles.

Level ✳. The stitched design is 58 x 58 stitches, approximately 10.5 x 10.5 cm (4¼ x 4¼ inches).

YOU WILL NEED:

* Fabric: 14 count Aida fabric in cream, 20 x 20 cm (8 x 8 inches)
* Tapestry needle: size 24
* Card mount: in brown
* Masking tape
* Wadding (optional)
* Thread: DMC 6-strand embroidery thread in the following colours and quantities:

Symbol	Colour	Shade	Skeins
✳	Dark Stone	646	1
◇	Mid Stone	642	1
●	Pale Stone	648	1
▲	Green	470	1

STITCHING INSTRUCTIONS

Cross stitch: Use three strands of embroidery thread.
Backstitch: Use two strands of dark stone.
Starting point: This is indicated on the chart on the right by an arrow. The first stitch should be made at a point 5 cm (2 inches) from the right-hand side and 5 cm (2 inches) from the bottom of the fabric.

MAKING UP

Iron the embroidery on the back on a thick towel. The dotted lines on the chart indicate the placement of the mount aperture. Buy or make a card mount to fit the size of your chosen frame. Here the aperture size is 13 x 13 cm (5 x 5 inches) and the outside measurement is 20 x 20 cm (8 x 8 inches). Centre the fabric carefully within the mount, trimming the Aida if necessary, and secure to the back of the mount with masking tape. It is very effective to pad the embroidered area slightly. To do this, cut a piece of wadding

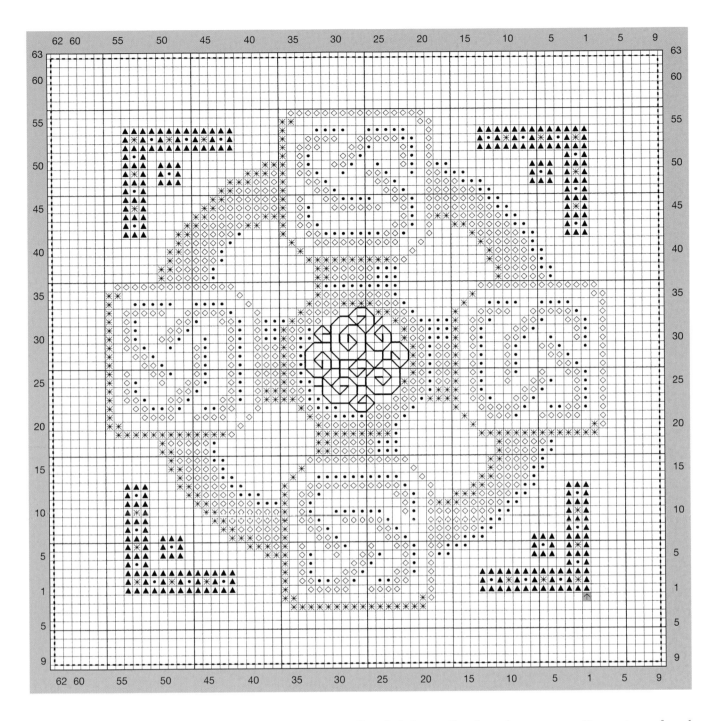

Chart legend:

- ✳ Dark Stone
- ◇ Mid Stone
- ● Pale Stone
- ▲ Green
- ↑ Start Point

slightly smaller than the aperture. Cut a piece of card the same size as the aperture. Place the wadding over the back of the embroidery, and the card on top of the wadding. Tape into place.

Variations

Use this design as a cushion centre and make up in the same way as the Spirals Cushion on page 91, adjusting the measurements to suit.

CELTIC CROSS CARD

Standing stones were linked with Celtic pagan sun cults. Just as Christian missionaries embraced and changed water cults into a Christian focus on healing wells, these stones became crosses and a focus for worship. Ordinary men were influenced by the beauty and story-telling powers of carved crosses.

Level ✱. The stitched design is 30 x 30 stitches, approximately 5.5 x 5.5 cm (2¼ x 2¼ inches).

YOU WILL NEED:

- Fabric: 14 count Aida fabric in cream, 13 x 13 cm (5 x 5 inches)
- Tapestry needle: size 24
- Steel rule and craft knife
- Card: in dark brown, cut to 11 x 22 cm (4¼ x 8½ inches)
- Stick glue or double-sided tape
- Thread: DMC 6-strand embroidery thread in the following colours and quantities:

Symbol	Colour	Shade	Skeins
✳	Dark Stone	646	1
◇	Mid Stone	642	1
●	Pale Stone	648	1
▲	Green	470	1

STITCHING INSTRUCTIONS

Cross stitch: Use three strands of embroidery thread.
Backstitch: Use two strands of dark stone.
Starting point: This is indicated on the chart by an arrow. The first stitch should be made at a point 3.5 cm (1½ inches) from the right-hand side and 3.5 cm (1½ inches) from the bottom of the fabric.

MAKING UP

Iron the embroidery on the back on a thick towel. The cutting line is four blocks out from the edge of the embroidery. Count out from the embroidery and carefully cut along the lines of the holes in the Aida. Fray back by two blocks, using the tip of a needle to tease out one thread at a time. Using a steel rule and a craft knife, lightly score and then fold the card to give a folded size of 11 x 11 cm (4¼ x 4¼ inches). Stick the embroidery centrally on the card using stick glue or double-sided tape.

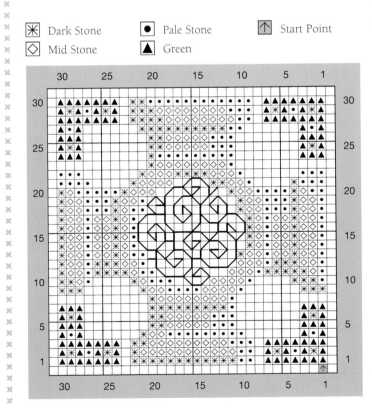

✳	Dark Stone	●	Pale Stone	↑	Start Point
◇	Mid Stone	▲	Green		

FABRIC CODES

FABRIC CODES:

The name given to fabric colours varies from supplier to supplier.

All the embroidery fabrics used in this book are manufactured by Zweigart & Sawitzki, and their codes are useful as standard source references.

11 count pale blue aida:	1007/503
14 count cream aida:	3706/264
14 count pale grey aida:	3706/713
14 count taupe aida:	3706/781
16 count dark grey aida:	3251/780
18 count cream aida:	3793/264
18 count dark red aida:	3793/969
27 count turquoise evenweave:	Meran 3972/574
28 count cream evenweave:	Cashel Linen 3281/101
28 count pale grey linen:	Cashel Linen 3281/718

AIDA BANDS:

3.5 cm (1½ inch) wide cream band:	7003/3
3.5 cm (1½ inch) wide white band:	7003/1
5 cm (2 inch) wide cream band:	7107/3
8 cm (3 inch) wide cream band:	7008/3

(5 cm (2 inch) wide gold band is exclusive to Textile Heritage Collection – see Suppliers on page 111)

DMC CHART
Quick reference table

Key to colour numbers:
Shade numbers on left, column numbers on right.

Shade	Col	Shade	Col	Shade	Col	Shade	Col	Shade	Col
ECRU	17	104	20	224	3	336	6	420	12
BLANC	17	105	20	225	3	340	5	422	12
B 5200	17	106	20	300	14	341	5	433	16
48	19	107	19	301	14	347	1	434	16
51	20	108	20	304	1	349	1	435	16
52	19	111	20	307	13	350	1	436	16
53	20	112	19	309	2	351	1	437	16
57	19	113	19	310	18	352	1	444	13
61	20	114	20	311	6	353	1	445	13
62	19	115	19	312	6	355	15	451	15
67	19	116	19	315	3	356	15	452	15
69	20	121	19	316	3	367	9	453	15
75	19	122	20	317	18	368	9	469	10
90	20	123	20	318	18	369	9	470	10
91	19	124	19	319	9	370	11	471	10
92	20	125	20	320	9	371	11	472	10
93	19	126	19	321	1	372	11	498	1
94	20	208	4	322	6	400	14	500	8
95	19	209	4	326	2	402	14	501	8
99	19	210	4	327	4	407	15	502	8
101	20	211	4	333	5	413	18	503	8
102	19	221	3	334	6	414	18	504	8
103	19	223	3	335	2	415	18	517	7

Shade	Col	Shade	Col	Shade	Col	Shade	Col	Shade	Col
518	7	744	13	906	10	3033	17	3787	17
519	7	745	13	907	10	3041	3	3790	16
520	10	746	12	909	9	3042	3	3799	18
522	10	747	7	910	9	3045	12	3801	1
523	10	754	15	911	9	3046	12	3802	3
524	10	758	15	912	9	3047	12	3803	3
535	17	760	1	913	9	3051	10	3804	4
543	16	761	1	915	4	3052	10	3805	4
550	4	762	18	917	4	3053	10	3806	4
552	4	772	9	918	14	3064	15	3807	5
553	4	775	6	919	14	3072	17	3808	7
554	4	776	2	920	14	3078	13	3809	7
561	8	778	3	921	14	3325	6	3810	7
562	8	780	12	922	14	3326	2	3811	7
563	8	781	12	924	8	3328	1	3812	7
564	8	782	12	926	8	3340	13	3813	8
580	11	783	12	927	8	3341	13	3814	8
581	11	791	5	928	8	3345	9	3815	8
597	7	792	5	930	6	3346	9	3816	8
598	7	793	5	931	6	3347	9	3817	8
600	4	794	5	932	6	3348	9	3818	9
601	4	796	5	934	10	3350	2	3819	11
602	4	797	5	935	10	3354	2	3820	12
603	4	798	5	936	10	3362	11	3821	12
604	4	799	5	937	10	3363	11	3822	12
605	4	800	5	938	16	3364	11	3823	13
606	13	801	16	939	6	3371	16	3824	13
608	13	806	7	943	8	3607	4	3825	14
610	12	807	7	945	14	3608	4	3826	14
611	12	809	5	946	13	3609	4	3827	14
612	12	813	5	947	13	3685	3	3828	12
613	12	814	1	948	15	3687	3	3829	12
632	15	815	1	950	15	3688	3	3830	15
640	17	816	1	951	14	3689	3	3831	2
642	17	817	1	954	9	3705	1	3832	2
644	17	818	2	955	9	3706	1	3833	2
645	17	819	2	956	2	3708	1	3834	3
646	17	820	5	957	2	3712	1	3835	3
647	17	822	17	958	7	3713	1	3836	3
648	17	823	6	959	7	3716	2	3837	4
666	1	824	5	961	2	3721	3	3838	5
676	12	825	5	962	2	3722	3	3839	5
677	12	826	5	963	2	3726	3	3840	5
680	12	827	5	964	7	3727	3	3841	6
699	10	828	5	966	9	3731	2	3842	7
700	10	829	11	970	13	3733	2	3843	6
701	10	830	11	971	13	3740	3	3844	6
702	10	831	11	972	13	3743	3	3845	6
703	10	832	11	973	13	3746	3	3846	6
704	10	833	11	975	14	3747	5	3847	7
712	16	834	11	976	14	3750	6	3848	7
718	4	838	16	977	14	3752	6	3849	7
720	14	839	16	986	9	3753	6	3850	8
721	14	840	16	987	9	3755	6	3851	8
722	14	841	16	988	9	3756	6	3852	12
725	13	842	16	989	9	3760	7	3853	14
726	13	844	17	991	8	3761	7	3854	14
727	13	869	12	992	8	3765	7	3855	14
729	12	890	9	993	8	3766	7	3856	14
730	11	891	2	995	6	3768	8	3857	15
731	11	892	2	996	6	3770	14	3858	15
732	11	893	2	3011	11	3772	15	3859	15
733	11	894	2	3012	11	3773	15	3860	15
734	11	895	9	3013	11	3774	15	3861	15
738	16	898	16	3021	17	3776	14	3862	16
739	16	899	2	3022	17	3777	15	3863	16
740	13	900	13	3023	17	3778	15	3864	16
741	13	902	3	3024	17	3779	15	3865	17
742	13	904	10	3031	16	3781	16	3866	17
743	13	905	10	3032	17	3782	17		

Exclusive numbering system of DMC © 2001

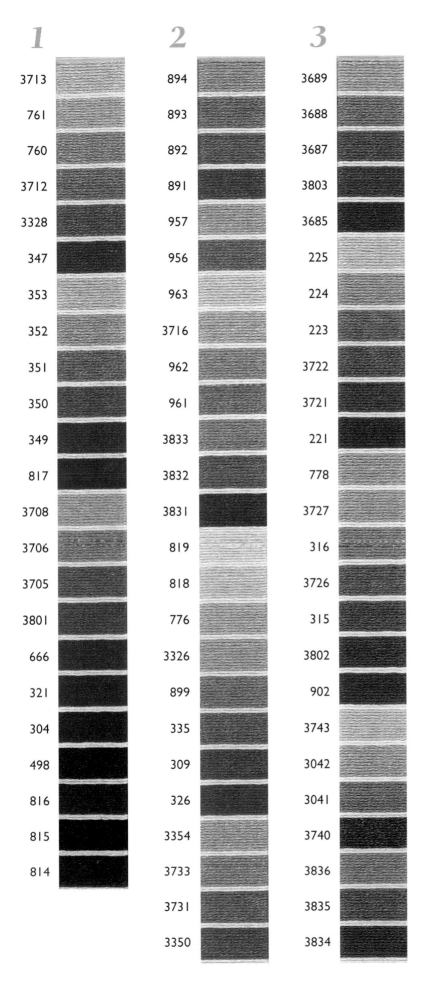
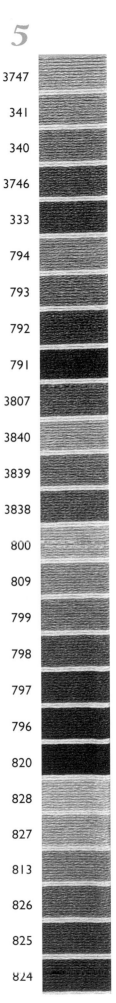

1	2	3	4	5
3713	894	3689	3806	3747
761	893	3688	3805	341
760	892	3687	3804	340
3712	891	3803	605	3746
3328	957	3685	604	333
347	956	225	603	794
353	963	224	602	793
352	3716	223	601	792
351	962	3722	600	791
350	961	3721	3609	3807
349	3833	221	3608	3840
817	3832	778	3607	3839
3708	3831	3727	718	3838
3706	819	316	917	800
3705	818	3726	915	809
3801	776	315	554	799
666	3326	3802	553	798
321	899	902	552	797
304	335	3743	550	796
498	309	3042	211	820
816	326	3041	210	828
815	3354	3740	209	827
814	3733	3836	208	813
	3731	3835	3837	826
	3350	3834	327	825
				824

Exclusive numbering system of DMC © 2001

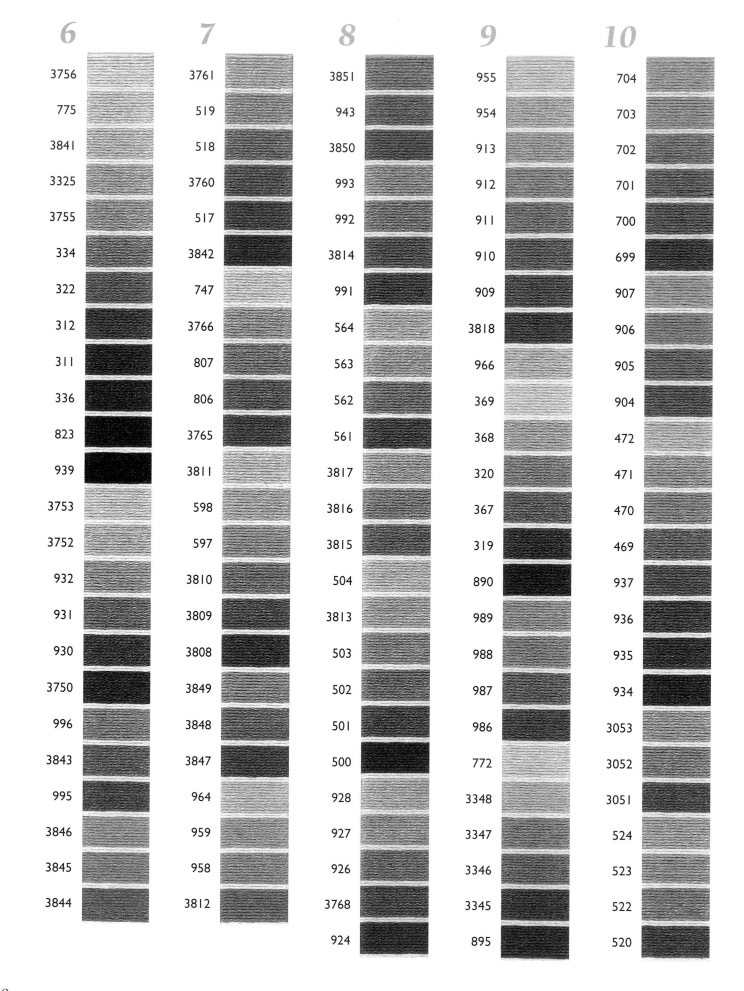

6	7	8	9	10
3756	3761	3851	955	704
775	519	943	954	703
3841	518	3850	913	702
3325	3760	993	912	701
3755	517	992	911	700
334	3842	3814	910	699
322	747	991	909	907
312	3766	564	3818	906
311	807	563	966	905
336	806	562	369	904
823	3765	561	368	472
939	3811	3817	320	471
3753	598	3816	367	470
3752	597	3815	319	469
932	3810	504	890	937
931	3809	3813	989	936
930	3808	503	988	935
3750	3849	502	987	934
996	3848	501	986	3053
3843	3847	500	772	3052
995	964	928	3348	3051
3846	959	927	3347	524
3845	958	926	3346	523
3844	3812	3768	3345	522
		924	895	520

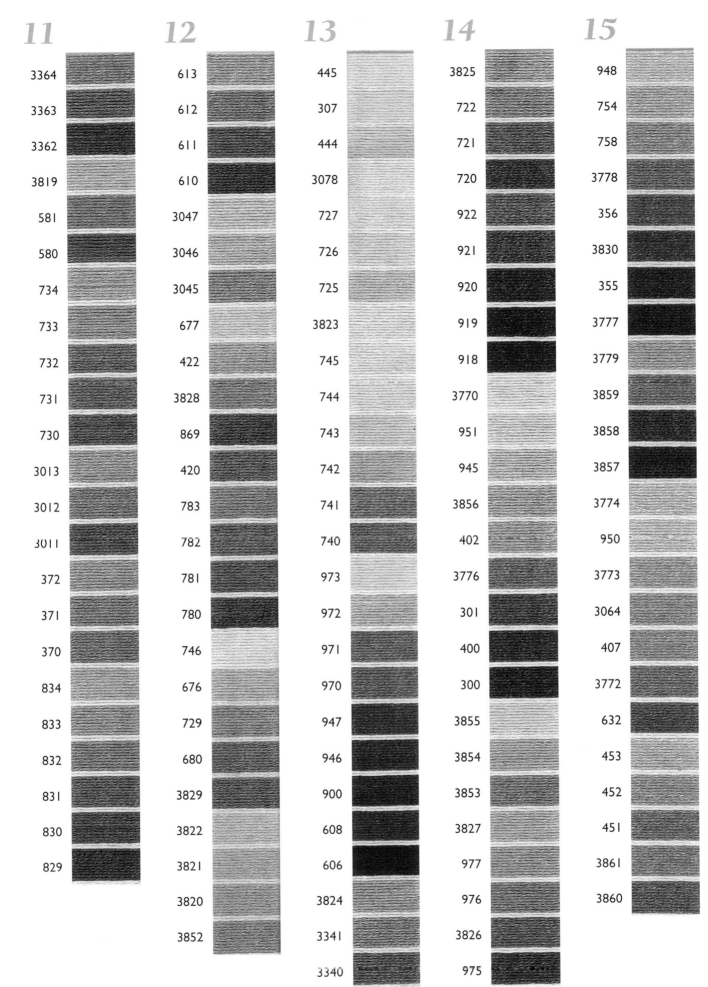

11	12	13	14	15
3364	613	445	3825	948
3363	612	307	722	754
3362	611	444	721	758
3819	610	3078	720	3778
581	3047	727	922	356
580	3046	726	921	3830
734	3045	725	920	355
733	677	3823	919	3777
732	422	745	918	3779
731	3828	744	3770	3859
730	869	743	951	3858
3013	420	742	945	3857
3012	783	741	3856	3774
3011	782	740	402	950
372	781	973	3776	3773
371	780	972	301	3064
370	746	971	400	407
834	676	970	300	3772
833	729	947	3855	632
832	680	946	3854	453
831	3829	900	3853	452
830	3822	608	3827	451
829	3821	606	977	3861
	3820	3824	976	3860
	3852	3341	3826	
		3340	975	

16

712
739
738
437
436
435
434
433
801
898
938
3371
543
3864
3863
3862
842
841
840
839
838
3790
3781
3031

17

B5200
BLANC
3865
ECRU
822
644
642
640
3866
3033
3782
3032
3024
3023
3022
3787
3021
3072
648
647
646
645
535
844

18

762
415
318
414
317
413
3799
310

19

48
116
62
112
107
57
75
115
99
95
126
52
102
124
93
113
121
103
67
91

20

123
125
101
114
122
92
94
104
90
108
51
106
111
61
105
69
53

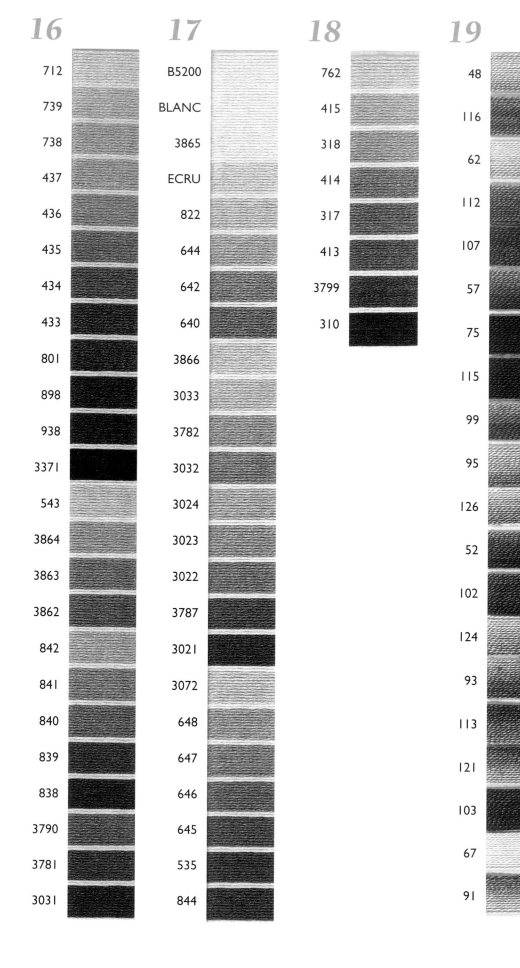
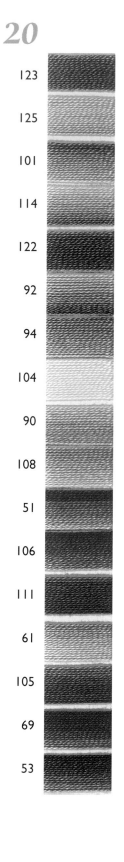

SUPPLIERS

UNITED KINGDOM

Most large department stores carry a good range of fabrics, threads and accessories. Look in the Yellow Pages under Art & Craft Equipment or Needlecraft Retailers.

DMC Creative World Ltd
Head Office
Pullman Road, Wigston
Leics LE18 2DY
Tel: 0116 281 1040
DMC threads can be found in branches of John Lewis nationwide. Phone for your nearest stockist.

Abakhan Fabrics
111-115 Oldham Street
Manchester M4 1LN
Tel: 0161 839 3229

Arts & Crafts Studios
14 St Michael's Row
Chester CH1 1EF
Tel: 01244 324900

B. Brown (Muraspec)
105-107 Dumbarton Road
Glasgow G11 6PW
Tel: 08705 340 340
e-mail:
customerservice@muraspec.com
web site: www.muraspec.com
Felt. Mail order only

Craft Creations
Ingersoll House
Delamare Road, Cheshunt
Herts EN8 9HD
Tel: 01992 781 900
e-mail:
enquiries@craftcreations.com
web site: www.craftcreations.com
Card blanks, tassels, etc. Mail order only

Creations
13 Market Hall
Inverness IV1 1PJ
Tel: 01463 241902

Creative Beadcraft
Denmark Works
Sheepcote Dell Road
Beamond End, Near Amersham
Bucks HP7 0RX
Tel: 01494 715 606
Beads. Mail order and stockists

David Morgan Ltd
26 The Hayes
Cardiff CF1 1UG
Tel: 029 2022 1011

The Embroidery Shop
51 William Street
Edinburgh EH3 7LW
Tel: 0131 225 8642

Fine Fabrics
Magdalene Lane
Taunton
Somerset TA1 1SE
Tel: 01823 270986

Framecraft Miniatures Ltd
372-376 Summer Lane
Hockley
Birmingham B19 3QA
Tel: 0121 212 0552
e-mail: sales@framecraft.com
web site: www.framecraft.com
Special boxes, brooches etc for embroidery. Mail order and stockists

Franklin & Sons
13a-15 St. Botolph's Street
Colchester
Essex CO2 7DU
Tel: 01206 563955

Liberty
Regent Street
London, W1R 6AH
Tel: 020 7225 5850

Pandora
196 High Street
Guildford
Surrey GU1 3HZ
Tel: 01483 572 558

Stitches
355 Warwick Road
Olton
Solihull B91 1BQ
Tel: 0121 706 1048

Sussex Needlecraft
37 Warwick Street
Worthing
E Sussex BN11 3DQ
Tel: 01903 823655

Textile Heritage Collection
5 India Buildings
Victoria Street
Edinburgh EH1 2EX
Tel: 0131 220 2420
e-mail:info@textileheritage.com
web site:
www.textileheritage.com
Special colours of Aida band. Mail order only

Willow Fabrics
95 Town Lane, Mobberley
Cheshire WA16 7HH
Tel: 0800 056 7811
e-mail:info@willowfabrics.com
web site: www.willowfabrics.com
Embroidery fabrics. Mail order only

SOUTH AFRICA

Cape Town Sewing Centre
78 Darling Street
Cape Town
Tel: (021) 465 2111

Johannesburg Sewing Centre
109 Pritchard Street
Johannesburg
Gauteng
Tel: (011) 333 3060

Sew & Save
Mimosa Mall
131 Brandwag
Bloemfontein
Tel: (051) 444 3122

Stitch Craft Centre
5 Umhlanga Centre Ridge
Ridge Road
Umhlanga Rocks
Durban
Tel: (031) 561 5822

Stitch Talk
Centurion Park
Centurion Square
Pretoria
Tel: (012) 663 2035

Thimbles & Threads
6 Quarry Centre
Hilton
Pietermaritzburg
Tel: (033) 43 1966

AUSTRALIA

Barbour Threads Pty Ltd
Suite E3, 2 Cowpasture Place
Wetherill Park
NSW 2164
Tel: (02) 9756 5466
Freecall: 1800 337 929

Birch Haberdashery and Craft
EC Birch Pty Ltd
Richmond
Victoria 3121
Tel: (03) 9429 4944

DMC Needlecraft Pty Ltd
51-55 Carrington Road
Marrickville
NSW 2204
Tel: (02) 9559 3088

Lincraft
Gallery level
Imperial Arcade
Pitt Street
Sydney
NSW 2000
Tel: (02) 9221 5111
(Stores nationwide)

Sewing Thread Specialists
41-43 Day Street (North)
Silverwater
NSW 2128
Tel: 1300 65 3855

Sullivans Haberdashery and
Craft Wholesalers
40 Parramatta Road
Underwood
Queensland 4119
Tel: (07) 3209 4799

NEW ZEALAND

The Embroiderer
140 Hinemoa Stree
Birkenhead
Auckland
Tel: (09) 419 0900

Nancy's Embroidery
273 Tinakori Road
Thorndon
Wellington
Tel: (04) 473 4047

Pauline's Needlecraft
94 Clyde Road
Browns Bay
Auckland
Tel: (09) 479 7783

Spotlight Stores
Carry a very large range of fabrics and haberdashery materials
Manukau - Tel: (09) 263 6760
or 0800 162 373
Wairau Park - Tel: (09) 444 0220
or 0800 224 123
Hamilton - Tel: (07) 839 1793
New Plymouth - Tel:
   (06) 757 3575
Wellington - Tel: (04) 472 5600
Christchurch - Tel:
   (03) 377 6121

Stitches
351 Colombo Street
Sydenham
Christchurch
Tel: (03) 379 1868
Email: stitches@xtra.co.nz

For a wider listing of embroidery suppliers nationwide, consult your Yellow Pages under 'Handcrafts & Supplies' or search under 'Shopping: Hobbies & Games: Handcrafts' on www.yellowpages.co.nz

INDEX

ANCHOR CONVERSION CHART

This conversion chart should only be used as a guide since it is not always possible to provide exact comparisons.

An * indicates that the Anchor shade has been used more than once and additional care should be taken to avoid duplication within a design.

DMC	Anchor	DMC	Anchor	DMC	Anchor	DMC	Anchor
B 5200	1	433	358	645	273	798	146
White	2	434	310	646	8581*	799	145
Ecru	387*	435	365	647	1040	800	144
208	110	436	363	648	900	801	359
209	109	437	362	666	46	806	169
210	108	444	291	676	891	807	168
211	342	445	28	677	361*	809	130
221	897*	451	233	680	901*	813	161*
223	895	452	232	699	923*	814	45
224	893	453	231	700	228	815	44
225	1026	469	267*	701	227	816	43
300	352	470	266*	702	226	817	13*
301	1049*	471	265	703	238	818	23*
304	19	472	253	704	256*	819	271
307	289	498	1005	712	926	820	134
309	42	500	683	718	88	822	390
310	403	501	878	720	326	823	152*
311	148	502	877*	721	324	824	164
312	979	503	876*	722	323*	825	162*
315	1019*	504	206*	725	305	826	161*
316	1017	517	1628	726	295*	827	160
317	400	518	1039	727	293	828	9159
318	235*	519	1038	729	890	829	906
319	1044*	520	862*	730	845*	830	277*
320	215	522	860	731	281*	831	277*
321	47	523	859	732	281*	832	907
322	978	524	858	733	280	833	874*
326	598	535	401	734	279	834	874*
327	1018	543	933	738	361*	838	1088
333	119	550	101*	739	366	839	1086
334	977	552	99	740	316*	840	1084
335	40*	553	98	741	304	841	1082
336	150	554	95	742	303	842	1080
340	118	561	212	743	302	844	1041
341	117	562	210	744	301	869	375
347	1025	563	208	745	300	890	218
349	13*	564	206*	746	275	891	35*
350	11	580	924	747	158	892	33*
351	10	581	281*	754	1012	893	27
352	9	597	1064	758	9575	894	26
353	8*	598	1062	760	1022	895	1044*
355	1014	600	59*	761	1021	898	380
356	1013*	601	63*	762	234	899	38
367	216	602	57	772	259	900	333
368	214	603	62*	775	128	902	897*
369	1043	604	55	776	24	904	258
370	888*	605	1094	778	968	905	257
371	887*	606	334	780	309	906	256*
372	887*	608	330*	781	308*	907	255
400	351	610	889	782	308*	909	923*
402	1047	611	898*	783	307	910	230
407	914	612	832	791	178	911	205
413	2368	613	831	792	941	912	209
414	235*	632	936	793	176	913	204
415	398	640	393	794	175	915	1029
420	374	642	392	796	133	917	89
422	372	644	391	797	132	918	341

DMC	Anchor	DMC	Anchor	DMC	Anchor
919	340	3047	852	3787	904*
920	1004	3051	845*	3790	904*
921	1003*	3052	844	3799	236*
922	1003*	3053	843	3801	1098
924	851	3064	883	3802	1019*
926	850	3072	397	3803	69
927	849	3078	292	3804	63*
928	274	3325	129	3806	62*
930	1035	3326	36	3807	122
931	1034	3328	1024	3808	1068
932	1033	3340	329	3809	1066*
934	862*	3341	328	3810	1066*
935	861	3345	268*	3811	1060
936	846	3346	267*	3812	188
937	268*	3347	266*	3813	875*
938	381	3348	264	3814	1074
939	152*	3350	77	3815	877*
943	189	3354	74	3816	876*
945	881	3362	263	3817	875*
946	332	3363	262	3818	923*
947	330*	3364	261	3819	278
948	1011	3371	382	3820	306
950	4146	3607	87	3821	305*
951	1010	3608	86	3822	295*
954	203*	3609	85	3823	386
955	203*	3685	1028	3824	8*
956	40*	3687	68	3825	323*
957	50	3688	75*	3826	1049*
958	187	3689	49	3827	311
959	186	3705	35*	3829	901*
961	76*	3706	33*	3830	5975
962	75*	3708	31	48	1207
963	23*	3712	1023	51	1220*
964	185	3713	1020	52	1209*
966	240	3716	25	57	1203*
970	925	3721	896	61	1218*
971	316*	3722	1027	62	1201*
972	298	3726	1018	67	1212
973	290	3727	1016	69	1218*
975	357	3731	76*	75	1206*
976	1001	3733	75*	90	1217*
977	1002	3740	872	91	1211
986	246	3743	869	92	1215*
987	244	3746	1030	93	1210*
988	243	3747	120	94	1216
989	242	3750	1036	95	1209*
991	1076	3752	1032	99	1204
992	1072	3753	1031	101	1213*
993	1070	3755	140	102	1209*
995	410	3756	1037	1103	1210*
996	433	3760	162*	104	1217*
3011	856	3761	928	105	1218*
3012	855	3765	170	106	1203*
3013	853	3766	167	107	1203*
3021	905*	3768	779	108	1220*
3022	8581*	3770	1009	111	1218*
3023	899	3772	1007	112	1201*
3024	388*	3773	1008	113	1210*
3031	905*	3774	778	114	1213*
3032	898*	3776	1048	115	1206*
3033	387*	3777	1015	121	1210*
3041	871	3778	1013*	122	1215*
3042	870	3779	868	124	1210*
3045	888*	3781	1050	125	1213*
3046	887*	3782	388*	126	1209*